50 MILES

Running the JFK, the Nation's Top Ultramarathon

by Dixie Shaffer

PHOTO CREDITS:

Cover and p. 13 photo of 2006 JFK 50 Mile start courtesy of Brightroom.com.

2007 winner photos on pp. 18 and 58 © Hagerstown Herald-Mail Co./Yvette May.

Ad on p. 7 and JFK photo on p. 10 from John F. Kennedy Presidential Library and Museum, Boston.

JFK 50 Mile event photos by Brenda Davidson on pp. 32, 46, and 47, and by Bunny Runyan on p. 59, courtesy of Anstr Davidson.

Alan and Pam Gowen, p. 28, courtesy of Alan Gowen.

Copyright © 2008 by Dixie Shaffer

ISBN 978-0-615-25153-0

Contents

Preface	5
Executive Decisions	7
2,250 Miles	13
The Runners	19
A New Perspective by Alan Gowen	29
The Course	33
Fifty Years	55
Resources	60
Appendix	62

Preface

I am not an ultramarathon runner. In fact, I've never run a marathon or any long-distance race. To be completely honest, running one mile on the treadmill leaves me winded. But that won't stop me from writing this book.

I am the daughter of an ultramarathon runner, a determined and driven man who took up running to keep in shape at an age when many men have less productive mid-life crises. One day, a friend razzed him, "You think you're a runner? I know a race you can't finish." Though the friend was teasing, my father took the challenge to heart, placing himself among the starters at the JFK 50 Mile Run in 1980. He arrived in Boonsboro wearing cutoff jeans and a T-shirt, clueless about how to dress and what to expect in the coming hours. Somewhere along the towpath, the course beat him soundly. It was a temporary defeat, which strengthened his resolve to cross the JFK finish line. Four years later—better trained and better prepared—Lloyd Storm succeeded.

Much of the background material for this book comes from my father's recollection of his many subsequent JFK 50 Mile runs. He is hooked. Of the subject, he does not tire. While accompanying me on a driving tour to most of the course checkpoints, he eagerly supplied details about the event.

While searching online for supplementary material, I was touched by the passion and fortitude of other JFK ultra runners. Many post online reports, candid accounts of their experiences. I was impressed that in the event's 45-year history, only two men have served as race director—the unstoppable founder and co-winner of the first JFK Challenge, Buzz Sawyer, and the man who succeeded him in style, two-time JFK champion Mike Spinnler. I was inspired by the RunnersWorld video of 13-year-old Mackenzie Riford's first attempt at the 50-miler, which she ran with her mother in 2007. After they crossed the finish line arm-in-arm, that young teen's face relayed a mix of disbelief, exhaustion and triumph that brought tears to my eyes.

The more I researched, the more I grew to respect the tremendous effort my father and others exert year after year to conquer this unique course. Some train solely for the JFK in the Fall; some run ultramarathons throughout the year—all take to the streets in bitter cold or sweltering heat alike to train, whether or not the timing is convenient. If you have a loved one training for the nation's largest ultramarathon, I hope this book gives you a deeper understanding of their persistence.

If you do not have a loved one consumed by this fire, chances are you know someone who is. While surfing through the lists of former JFK finishers on the event's Web site, JFK50mile.org, I was surprised to find two former classmates—Edward "Skip" Tovornik and Warren "Butch" Shingleton; a former co-worker, Darrell Hull; and a neighbor, Courtney Campbell, who is among the top 10 all-time JFK performers. If you did not attend Washington County schools as I did, maybe you are an alternative rock fan who will appreciate that Goo Goo Dolls drummer Mike Malinin was among the finishers at JFK 2007.

I am not an ultramarathon runner. I handled my own mid-life crisis by going back to school. My finish line was a bachelor's degree, a race hammered out by my fingertips on a keyboard. This desk-bound endeavor left me well below President Kennedy's ideal of a physically fit American. Yet my path required fortitude; I can fathom a runner's perseverance in working toward a goal and the thrill of reaching it.

If you are not an ultramarathon runner, I hope you will gain from this book not only an appreciation of the JFK 50 Mile Run—the nation's oldest and largest ultramarathon—but also a glimpse of the excitement a runner feels stepping over the start at Boonsboro and the exhaustion and elation that follows placing one foot in front of the other more times than one can count to cover fifty miles.

—Dixie Shaffer
Sept. 2, 2008

Executive Decisions

The John F. Kennedy 50-Mile Challenge

The JFK 50 Mile takes place each November, starting on the National Pike in Boonsboro, Md.; the historical starting point, however, is in the early 1960s in a place that some call Camelot.

John F. Kennedy championed a vigorous lifestyle during an era when red flags were waving over poor physical fitness. Even before the youngest president took office, mechanization rapidly was replacing mundane, time-consuming tasks. The fifties ushered in the all-electric kitchen and laundry room, the automatic dishwasher, refrigerator defroster and washing machine—all controlled by the flick of a switch. While the objects around them sped up, Americans slowed down. Rather than exercising their muscles with a long walk to school or to the store, they hopped in the car. The automated world moved on, leaving in its wake free time, which young and old alike often filled with television-watching or other sedentary pursuits. The detrimental effect of inactivity on one's physical well-being was not a common topic of discussion. Enlightening the public required presidential intervention.

The President's Council on Physical Fitness and Sports credits Dr. Hans Kraus with raising an early warning about the declining physical condition of Americans. According to their article, "History of the President's Council on Physical Fitness and Sports (1956–2006)," * Kraus and his associates administered a series of muscular fitness tests to thousands of children and found that more than half of American youth failed at least one of the tests, compared to less than 10 percent of Europeans. This was unacceptable. A national epidemic. Kraus's findings captured the attention of President Eisenhower, whose administration could verify the scope of the problem: Roughly half of the men presented to the draft office were deemed unfit to serve. Eisenhower responded by creating the President's Council on Youth Fitness to persuade and educate the public about the importance of good physical health.

> "I've got Donelap Disease," said the comedian, patting his round midsection. "My stomach done lap over my belt."
> —Clear Spring Minstrel Show joke, 1978

President Kennedy took the previous administration's campaign and rocked it—that is, took it to the next level. Media-savvy JFK made physical fitness a hot topic as well as "a defining principle of his administration," according to the Council. Before taking office, Kennedy outlined his policy in an article "The Soft American," published in Sports Illustrated.

Kennedy's program would do more than persuade and educate Americans; it would publish information and provide advice to help them to achieve physical fitness. The Kennedy Council conducted this campaign in conjunc-

---

* The main text of the article is reprinted in the Appendix.

tion with the National Advertising Council to produce material for print, radio, and television. An article in the JFK Presidential Library and Museum, "The Federal Government Takes on Physical Fitness," called Kennedy's ad campaign organized and extensive. One ad posed the question, "Is this the shape of things to come?" alongside a man's distended midsection. The ad blamed "easy living" for "sapping the strength and vitality of our children."

The media blitz worked, electrifying Americans to accept a presidential challenge that was not directed to them, and led ultimately to the birth of the JFK 50 Mile Run. As the story goes, Kennedy learned of a presidential directive from Theodore Roosevelt who required his officers to march 50 miles in 20 hours, "double-timing the last 700 yards," according to *Time* maga-

I think it's time America started moving again.

—John F. Kennedy

zine (February 15, 1963). Kennedy indicated to Marine Commandant David M. Shoup that if his marine officers could match these requirements, Kennedy would see to the fitness of his own White House staff. Shoup promptly sent on this fitness mission North Carolina marine officers "in dungarees, boots, helmets and 24-lb. packs," according to *Time*. The first marine to cover 50 miles did so in less than 12 hours.

True to his word, Kennedy raised the issue with his White House staff, prompting a seemingly enthusiastic* response from his brother. On February 9, 1963, Attorney General Robert Kennedy rose before dawn to traipse along the snow-covered C & O Canal towpath. A *Life* magazine photo portrays Bobby taking a break somewhere between Great Falls and Camp David with his walking companion and dog, Brumis. Bobby completed the 50 miles in less than 18 hours while wearing his leather Oxford shoes.

Considering the media coverage these events garnered, it is not surprising that the public took the challenge personally. After all, it was the American people whose physiques were being disparaged. Neither the President nor the

---

* For an amusing account of Bobby's reaction, read what Edwin Guthman, his press aide, had to say at www.people.com/people/archive/article/0,,20099135,00.html

> We want a nation of participants in the vigorous life. This is not a matter which can be settled, of course, from Washington. It is really a matter which starts with each individual family. . . .
>
> —President John F. Kennedy, 1961
> Conference on Physical Fitness of Youth

fitness council suggested that the public cover such long distances; nevertheless, 50-mile hikes soon were organized throughout the country. So persuasive was the Kennedy charisma that only one week after the initial report, a follow-up article in *Time* noted the growing popularity of these hikes among Boy Scouts, college fraternities, and reporters eager for a feature story with a personal twist.

The 50-mile hikes were carried out on a local level, initiated by local individuals who championed the cause. In Hagerstown, Md., that person was Buzz Sawyer, the founder of the Cumberland Valley Athletic Club (CVAC) and a renowned distance runner who specialized in the two-mile run and coached high school runners during the off-season. Jumping with both feet on the fitness bandwagon, Sawyer mapped out his JFK 50-Mile Challenge, a route through Washington County that would keep runners out of traffic, according to a *Herald-Mail* article by Janet Heim (2002). An unexpected byproduct of Sawyer's charting off the beaten path was an extremely challenging course.

> Only those who dare to fail greatly, can ever achieve greatly.
>
> —Robert F. Kennedy, June 6, 1966

The first event took place on March 30, 1963—two months after Bobby Kennedy's extended stroll along the towpath. Eleven CVAC members participated and four finished: Sawyer along with Steve Cosition, James Ebberts, and Rick Miller. Clocking in together at 13:10, they beat Kennedy's time limit by nearly seven hours.

The 50-mile craze came to an unexpected end on November 22, 1963, when Kennedy was assassinated. Reeling from the shock, the country lost heart for the hikes. Buzz Sawyer, however, was not a quitter. He made an executive decision to hold a second 50-miler in 1964, renaming it the JFK 50-Mile Memorial in honor of the fallen president. Sixteen people took part in the quest and seven achieved it. The three co-winners shaved 37 minutes off of the winning time, establishing a trend that would continue over the next four decades as the trek evolved into a race, rather than a hike.

By continuing the event, Sawyer carried out the wishes of a President who encouraged Americans not only to take action to improve physical fitness but also to strive for excellence in all areas. By carrying on, Sawyer answered the question posed by Kennedy's ad "Is this the shape of things to come?" with a resounding "No!" Each runner who logs 50 JFK miles adds a voice to this response.

JFK 2006 start. Photo courtesy of Brightroom.com

2,250 Miles

JFK 50 Mile Run
1963-2007

On November 18, 2006, 1,154 runners stepped over the starting line in downtown Boonsboro to begin their 50-mile tour of Washington County. Those who were properly prepared, those who didn't take a tumble on the Appalachian Trail or give in to the boredom and physical exhaustion of the C & O Canal towpath, would reach the finish line—1,017 in all, reaffirming the JFK's status as the nation's largest ultramarathon. From Pete Breckinridge of Norfolk, Va., to John Worley of Columbia, Md., this class of the JFK graduated in less than 14 hours and covered a combined 50,850 miles, a distance that wraps the earth twice. Breckinridge, a 36-year-old who clocked in at 6:04:40, was followed by eighteen others who also took less than seven hours to accomplish the feat. It was fitting that the CVAC could boast another banner year in 2006, the 50th anniversary of the President's Council on Physical Fitness and Sports.

Even a visionary like Kennedy would have had trouble foreseeing the long-term effect of his fitness campaign, raging stronger than ever in the 21st century. Propelled by the strength of those eight tired legs that completed the course in 1963, the JFK 50 Mile has grown exponentially during its 45-year history to tally a staggering 18,014 finishers and a total 900,700 miles. Covered on foot, one step at a time, this distance is nearly equal to the length of two round trips to the moon.

> **A journey of a thousand miles begins with one step.**
> —Chinese proverb

Such is the momentum that can build from the actions of one person with strength of character and determination, whether a president or a long-distance runner. In these days of quick turnovers of business managers, sports coaches and even personal relationships, only two men have served as race director of the JFK 50-Mile: Buzz Sawyer (1963–92) and Mike Spinnler (1993 to present).

Directing a race of this magnitude is not an easy task and the thousands of participants are not the only concerns. When your course cuts a 50-mile swath through national parks and landmarks, towns and neighborhoods, you must work with government officials as well as local citizens. In doing so over the years, Sawyer and Spinnler have adjusted course starting and stopping points and times. They have shortened Kennedy's original time allowance for the 50 miles to 15 hours, then later to only 12 to meet requirements of the National Park Service that runners exit the towpath by 5 p.m. To appease runners who do not expect to finish in 12 hours, Spinnler established an alternate 5 a.m. start, allowing two more hours to complete the race. According to the CVAC's 2008 pre-race packet, the early start is limited to 250 people who must submit written requests in advance for approval by race officials.

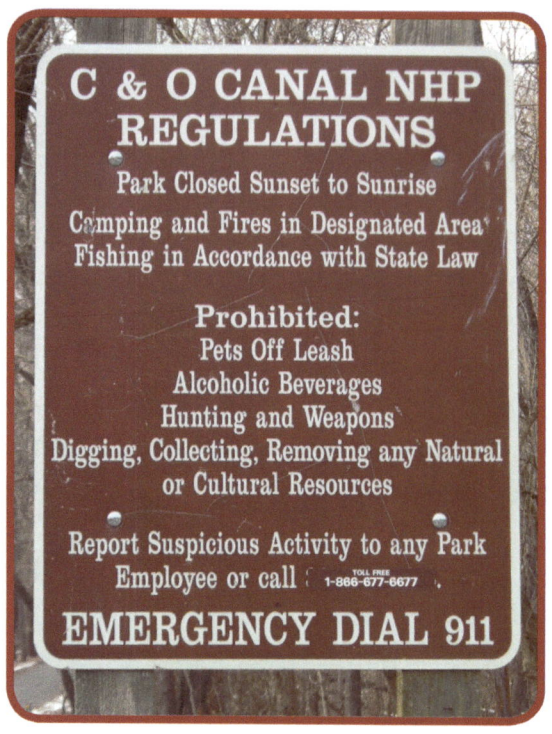

This sign at Dam 4 marks the end of the towpath segment and reminds runners they must hit the pavement by sunset.

The CVAC notes, "Most well-prepared 4:00 marathoners finish the JFK 50 Mile in the 10-hour range."

As if these myriad human concerns were not enough, race officials also must contend with Mother Nature. Originally held in the spring, the JFK changed to a fall event in 1975 to lessen the likelihood that runners would be pelted with rain. This inspired move was tested 10 years later on race day when the canal was flooded. The timing of the change in seasons coincided with a leveling off in the number of race entrants. Could this decline be attributed to lower temperatures? Cold had become a major factor. While those running JFK on April Fool's Day 1967 enjoyed 80-degree weather, those running a week before Thanksgiving 1987 grappled with a wind chill factor of minus 15 degrees.

In the early years of Sawyer's 50-miler, participation grew slowly, according to the Statistical Datelines chart on JFK50mile.org; however, 1969 was a turning point. That year, the number of finishers doubled to 40 and co-winners James Ebberts and Baxter Berryhill shaved a full hour and a half from the course record (8:32:04). The next year, Berryhill crossed the finish solo, bettering his previous time by more than one hour. In 1971, Elton Horst improved the record by yet another hour. Two years later, Max White was the first to break the six-hour barrier. White finished in 5:55:30, and there was no turning back: all subsequent winning times remained around the six-hour mark. During the ensuing years, a dozen more runners completed the race in five hours plus change.

The string of course records and stellar performances added to the ultramarathon's prestige and the excitement it generated. Before the event changed seasons, participation doubled annually from 1970–73, when 1,724 runners started the race—the most in U.S. ultra history, according to JFK50mile.org. By this time, women had joined the fray, led by Donna Aycoth, the race's top female finisher from 1968–73. Aycoth capped off her reign with a personal record (PR) of 8:26:07—faster than any winning time in the 1960s.

After the heydays of the early 1970s, participation dropped slightly and then leveled off. During the next twenty years, JFK officials counted an average 300 finishers per event. Participation numbers remained steady while runners continued to excel. Mike Spinnler, for example, had back-to-back wins, setting in 1982 a course record of 5:53:05 which remained unbroken for 12 years and is to date the best time achieved by a Washington County resident.

A pivotal year for the JFK 50 Mile was 1994. Participation numbers once again were on the rise. Eric Clifton set a new course record of 5:46:22, which remains unbeaten in 2007. This took place shortly after founder Buzz Sawyer, the driving force behind 32 consecutive events, had handed over the reins of the nation's oldest ultramarathon to one of its champions, Mike Spinnler.

Under Spinnler's supervision, the 50-miler continued to grow into the nation's largest, counting by 2005 a total 952 finishers—the most in U.S. ultra history. This total was surpassed in 2006 and eclipsed in 2007 when 1,078 men, women and youth crossed the JFK finish line. Their combined mileage could start a third trip around the world.

At sunrise on Saturday, November 17, 2007, runners from 46 different states and Canada crowded behind the starting line. Three minutes later, when the gun sounded, 33-year-old Michael Wardian of Arlington, Va., headed toward his first ultramarathon victory. Wardian posted 5:50:34, the only time under six hours in JFK 2007 and the second fastest in event history.

Sixteen runners followed Wardian to an under-seven-hour finish: 15 men, including 2006 champion Breckinridge, and Anne Lundblad, the number one woman and 11th runner overall. Lundblad holds the woman's course record of 6:29:42, set in 2005. "She's one of the three or four best ultramarathoners in the U.S. and the best at 50 miles," Spinnler commented in a *Frederick NewsPost* report by Karen Gardner.

As the sun set on the 45th annual JFK, Daniel Fossier, 39, stepped over the finish line. This runner from Decatur, Ill., was the 407th to cross, leaving more than half of the field to follow beneath a darkening sky. Two minutes before the official end of the race, Richard Wong, 49, crossed the finish. This Springfield, Va., runner was the last to conquer the course, and he did so six hours faster than Kennedy's 20-hour challenge.

Anne Lundblad flies toward another first-place finish in the JFK 50 Mile women's division (2007).

The Runners

Profile of the
JFK 50-Miler

Who is the JFK runner? Although the typical runner is likely to be a 42-year-old male from Maryland who has finished the race before, this 50-miler attracts a diverse group of men and women from throughout the United States and Canada. To exclude the bulk of the population from this description, consider who the JFK runner is not. He or she is not less than 13 years old, not obesely overweight, an armchair athlete, undisciplined or unmotivated.

Crowded behind the starting line, the forest of athletes appear remarkably similar. Physically fit, their trunks wrapped in running apparel, they are rooted in a common mission. But as the race progresses, individuals emerge—young and old, men and women, with varying levels of experience and ability. Experience will influence the choices each makes during the race; ability, training and a measure of luck determine the outcome.

A runner's expectations for finishing the race shape his or her overall goal, which assumes one of two forms. A runner can compete for either place or time. In 2007, Andy Mason, 35, of Hagerstown, trained to crack the top 10, while Alan Downs, 19, of Clear Spring, was one of the many who opted to race the clock, aiming to break 9.5 hours on his second JFK run. Another clockwatcher was Alan Gowen, 57, who looked for a time of less than 10 hours as did father and son running partners David and Kevin Grimm. Lloyd Storm, 67, claims his chief goal each year is simply to finish and keep his streak going: "I've had so many times I've lost focus and slowed down, that to stay consistent throughout this event is my primary goal." But those who know Storm understand he will not be satisfied, unless he has given the race all he's got. Or has beaten his longtime running rival. He admits, "Of course, if I can finish ahead of Paul, that is only icing on the cake."

> [The profile of a JFK runner:] . . . those who seek a unique experience, have a love for the sport, look for the ultimate challenge, and accept the risk of failure and/or injury.
>
> —George Banker, JFK50mile.org

The rival is Paul Betker, 62, who has completed 26 back-to-back JFK 50 Mile runs, which is why Storm and the others in their running group see Betker as a worthy competitor. Like a moving game of Where's Waldo? they play Where's Paul? searching throughout the race for the blue shirt with white stripes. Whether they perceive Paul to be ahead or behind, the incentive is the same, propelling them forward to either catch up to or stay ahead of Paul.

Grimm paints a humorous picture of his encounter with Betker at the last event. "We saw Paul at the start. He looks the same every year—blue shirt with the stripes and New Balance shoes. I asked him how he expects to do. He gave me the usual Paul response—'Don't know, just going to do what I can, not where I want to be with my training, can't tell you my training secrets' . . . I think he likes the psychological warfare."

For an individual sport, ultramarathons are remarkably social. Friendships tied to a time of physical exhaustion, pain, and personal triumph are friendships that last. Like making it through high school with a best friend or surviving boot camp with a pal.

Divine intervention provided Alan Gowen the opportunity to reflect on the social aspect of the race. Having completed 11 ultras with 5 PRs in 2007, Gowen was in the best condition of his life and eagerly anticipated the JFK. He expected to set a PR in the race, a realistic goal, considering his performance during the year. Ever-diligent with his training, on Saturday of Labor Day weekend Gowen ran 27.5 miles on the Tuscarora Trail; on Sunday, he bicycled 50 miles; on Monday, he played tennis and . . . tore his hamstring. Sidelined for JFK 2007, Gowen and his wife Pam—also a temporarily out-of-commission ultrarunner—gained a "new perspective" about the race. Read his story on page 29.

While anyone running to place must limit camaraderie during the race, those running for time have a choice to make. Do I run solo or with a partner? Again, the runner's overall goal dictates the answer. Alongside self-imposed time limits, many runners simultaneously hope to achieve a PR by finishing the 50-mile journey more quickly than before. This is difficult to accomplish while running with another, since individuals have different strides, get tired and hungry at different times and fall into different run–walk patterns. Anyone who chooses to run with a partner invariably will be stalled by that person at one time or another. Kevin Sayers, director of the Catoctin 50K in Frederick, Md., wrote on this subject, "Everyone has different highs and lows and they usually don't sync with your partner."

Consider Elton Horst, who finished JFK 1965 in 10:39 with running pals Buzz Sawyer and James Ebberts. The next year, Horst completed the course in 10:21 with Sawyer and Kenny Baker. Presumably, Horst enjoyed these treks with his companions, yet during that first decade, the JFK evolved from a hike into a race. Proving the point in the 9th annual event, held April 3, 1971, Elton Horst ran full out and crossed the finish line solo in 6:15:42—the first JFK finish in less than seven hours. Although he logged a respectable time of 7:42:03, second-place runner Sam Holland came in a full hour-and-a-half behind Horst.

Yet even those committed to going it alone can benefit from a friend in need. During his first JFK, Alan Downs suffered on the towpath with severe muscle cramps which forced him to slow to a walk for about an hour. Downs recalls he might not have finished the race without help: ". . . my buddy Tom

Louderback, who I'd run with on the AT, caught up with me. He pulled me out of my rut and got me to start running again."

Racing partners provide moral support and push each other to excel. The youngest entrants in 2007, 13-year-olds Kevin Grimm and Mackenzie Riford, had their running-partner parents to thank for escorting them across the finish line. Married couples might go the course alone but join later to swap war stories. Mark and Anne Lundblad of Ashville, N.C., for example, are tough competitors who do not finish hand-in-hand. Mark is a 50-mile national champion who placed fourth in JFK 2007 (6:09:17).

> **At the first AID STATION—I had to correct Kevin when he called them REST STOPS...**
> —David Grimm on running the JFK 50 Mile with his 13-year-old son

CATEGORIES OF RUNNERS

JFK finishers are categorized by age and sex and by whether they run individually or as part of a declared team. While each finisher receives a medal, the CVAC recognizes during an awards ceremony the top 10 men, top 5 women, and the first man and woman in each of six age groups: 13–19, 40–49, 50–59, 60–69, 70–79, and 80+. Awards are also presented to the top performing male, female and military teams.

The competition for a top spot is not as great for women. During the last 12 events, women accounted for about 20 percent of all participants, with more at age 39 than at any other. The most common age for a male runner is 50, although more runners are in their forties than any other age group, as Mike Spinnler noted in a Planet Ultramarathon article. For some men, the race seems to be a rite of passage, evidenced by participation peaks at age 21, 40, 45 and 50. (See chart on the next page.) The oldest runner was Carl Llewellyn of Hagerstown, who finished JFK 1995 when he was 80 years old (13:45:57). These days, Llewellyn keeps his ninety-something body in shape with two-mile runs on the C & O Canal Towpath.

Lead runners tend to be a few years younger than the norm. The 100 best finishers from 1996–2007 were an average 35 years old. Ninety-nine of these are men and one is a woman—the amazing Anne Lundblad, who at age 39 ran the 50 miles faster than any other woman in event history and all but 68 men in the 12-year sample.

Directly above Lundblad in this top 100 ranking is 50-year-old Tim Hewitt of Greensburg, Pa. Although he is the oldest runner in this group, Hewitt's name appears on the list more than once, as do the names of 21 others. The most frequent entry is Ian Torrence of Boulder City, Nev., who finished in less than 8 hours each year from 1997–2005. At 27 in 1999, Torrence set his PR of 6:09:27, earning him a 19th-place ranking during this time period.

While finishing ahead of the pack is a sure sign of superior stamina, it is also an indication of how well one has addressed more practical matters, like training, gear and nutrition.

TRAINING

A more accurate title for this book would be The *Final* 50 Miles, since completing an ultramarathon, while an awesome accomplishment, is but the last 50 miles of exponentially more. Exactly how many miles a runner covers while training depends on one's ultimate race goal, which must be rooted in reality. Neither a 13- nor a 70-year-old expects to place first and typically trains at a level that conditions the body to cross the finish line within a self-imposed time limit.

Time devoted to school assignments and other activities tempers the training plan of younger runners. Thirteen-year-old Kevin Grimm followed a regimen set by his father who managed to work into their busy schedules each week from late January through October a long run, long bike ride, mountain

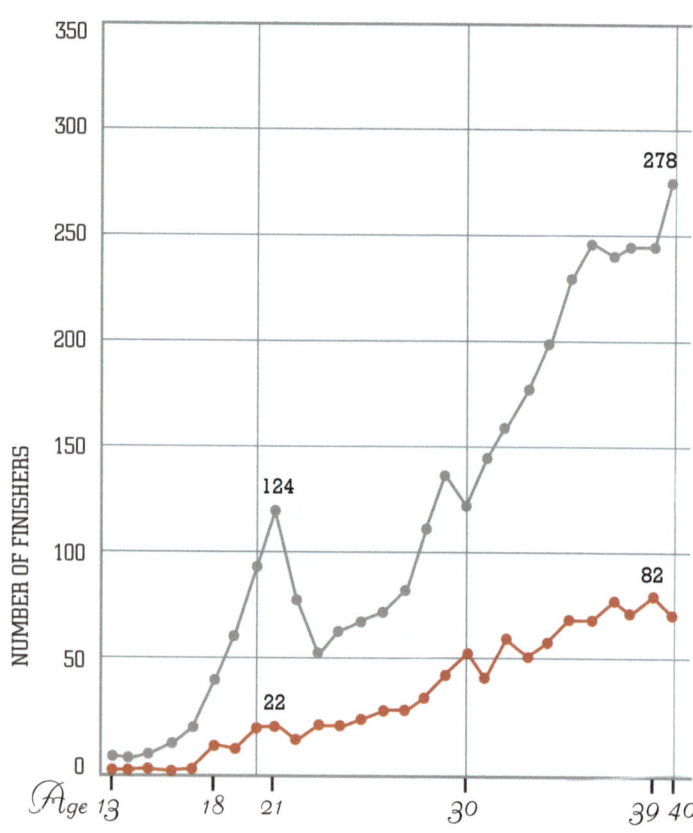

JFK Finishers 1996–2007 by Age

There seems to be something magic about turning 50 and running the JFK 50 Mile.
—Mike Spinnler in *Planet Ultramarathon*

run and mountain bike ride. Six years Grimm's senior, Alan Downs prepped for the race by running 8–10 miles a day. Assuming he ran 50 miles a week for 40 weeks, Downs had 2,000 miles under his belt by the time he reached downtown Boonsboro in November.

At the other end of the spectrum are runners aged sixty-plus. Rather than seeking out time, these runners attempt to escape the ravages of it or at least to overcome time's toll on their physiques. They adjust training plans to match the amount of abuse the body can endure. Storm likens training for "geezers" to "walking a fence, a balancing act whereby you either fall over to the overtrained and injured side or the undertrained side." He fell off of the fence in late October 2006 during a run on the Rails to Trails. His legs felt increasingly heavy, making him wonder, "Am I now too old to cut the mustard? Is this the best I can do?" Determined to pull out of the slump, he inserted two more Appalachian Trail (AT) runs into his pre-JFK schedule. His body rebelled against the punishment, and the "dead legs syndrome" resurfaced. To add injury to insult, Storm slipped on a wet, flat rock, fell on his shoulder and bumped his head on another rock. Luckily, he joked, his shoulder broke the fall so that the rock was not damaged: "The park service frowns on habitat destruction, right?"

> Time, time, time
> See what's become of me
> While I looked around
> For my possibilities.
> —Paul Simon, *Hazy Shade of Winter*

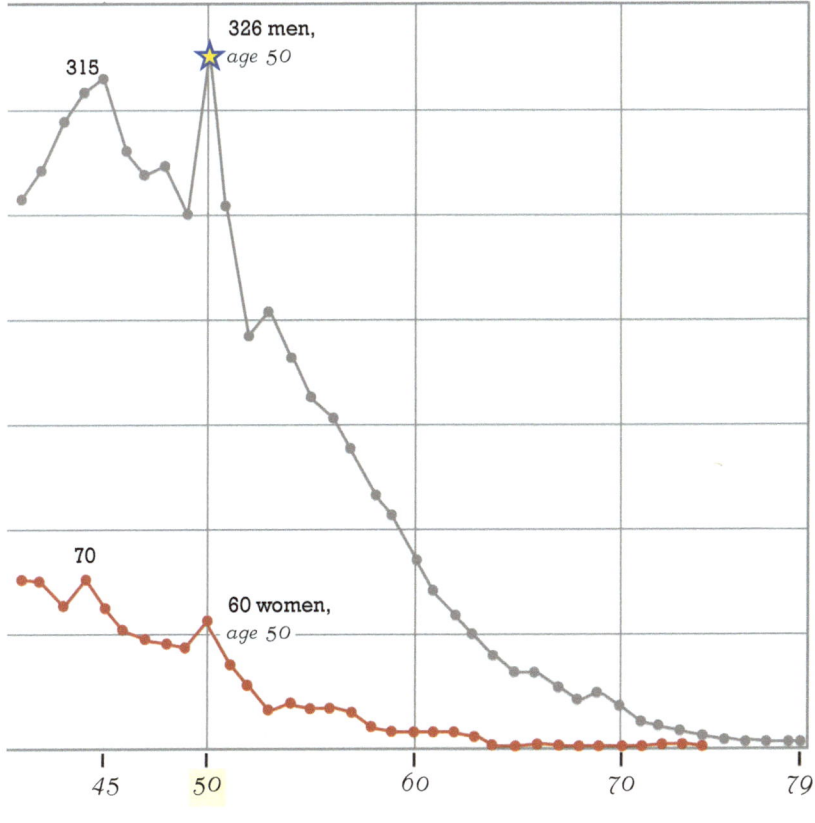

Perseverance, accompanied by minor concessions to age, can allow a runner to triumph over injuries. Conceding ever so slightly in 2007, Storm decreased his weekly runs to 45 miles.* The strategy worked. His training peaked in early November, enabling him to finish the JFK in 10:10—42 minutes faster than in 2006 and ahead of younger competitors, including GooGoo Dolls drummer Mike Malinin, 40, who was himself recovering from an injury.

Although Grimm, Downs, and Storm gear their training programs toward the JFK 50 Mile in the fall, others enjoy running ultramarathons throughout the year. In 2006, Gowen took on one ultra each month, including a 100-miler, the Massanutten Mountain Trails. This grueling schedule affected how he would have normally prepared for the JFK. ". . . because of my one-ultra-a-month schedule, I really hadn't trained for JFK like I felt I should. All year long I had either been recovering after or tapering before that month's race, not leaving much time for any quality training. In fact in the two weeks prior to JFK I had chosen to not run even one step . . ." Gowen set a realistic goal of finishing the JFK in less than 10 hours. Despite his pre-race lethargy, the monthly dose of ultra-running enabled Gowen to meet his target with a 9:52:45 finish in JFK 2006.

> **I trained harder for this year's JFK than any other race in my life. Over September and October, I only missed one day of running. In October, I logged 346 miles—an average of 11.2 per day.**
> —Andy Mason, Herald-Mail.com

If covering a ton of miles during training seems intense, consider the ramped-up schedule of a top finisher. In the spirit of the 50-mile hikes in 1963 when reporters participated to lend their stories a personal touch, Andy Mason wrote about his JFK 2007 run for the Hagerstown *Herald-Mail*. According to his article, Mason trained to place at the head of the pack, logging in October alone a whopping 346 miles, sufficient conditioning for a top 10 finish. Mason placed ninth with a time of 6:39:09.

Along with scheduling training sessions to meet realistic goals, JFK runners must consider the varying terrain they will encounter. This means gaining experience with footing on uneven surfaces, covering steep inclines and practicing on downhill runs to build the quad muscles. It also means training in a climate similar to the one likely to be in Washington County on a mid-Fall morning: cold, maybe wet, possibly freezing.

---

* Even with this less stringent goal, Storm's pedometer totals by November a whopping 1,800 miles—a pre-race jaunt roughly the distance from the Appalachians to the Rockies.

GEAR

An important part of race planning includes gear considerations. The usual Pre-Thanksgiving weather is cold, yet runners can not discount the chance of an unseasonably warm day. Shorts or pants? That's the first clothes-related question. A novice runner is unlikely to own top-of-the-line sportswear—Storm started his first JFK in cutoff Wranglers—yet most are able to round up a pair of Nike running shorts. The veteran is apt to recite a litany of preferred apparel that would rival any red-carpet celebrity's outfit report to the press. Check out Will Brown's gear list for JFK 1996:

> Capilene long sleeve shirt, windproof jacket . . . long sleeve mock turtleneck with bib . . . Shorts and Sporthills . . . Bill Rogers hat and heavy duty Thermaloft mittens.

Race veteran Vic Culp dressed in a long-sleeve Coolmax shirt and singlet, neck gaiter, knit hat and shorts. He wore trail shoes at the start, but changed into Air Max after getting off the AT and into a lighter weight road shoe at mile 43.

Culp's strategy raises the second gear-related issue for pre-race deliberation: To change or not to change? Shoes, that is. Many opt to do so at least once. The Grimm duo laced up fresh footwear at Weverton and again at Shepherdstown. Many find that wearing a lightweight shoe for the final leg of the race along the pavement helps them to a strong finish. Others, however, need the ankle support provided by a heavier shoe.

Additional gear changes are sometimes necessary. Anyone fortunate enough to have a handler, family member or friend along the course can plan to have extra supplies available. David Grimm had the forethought to pack extra gloves, which his son needed at Weverton: "Kevin's hands were freezing and he was having trouble tying his shoes. Somehow, his gloves had gotten wet and his fingers were numb."

The mantra for an ultrarunner organizing clothes and equipment is "Do not introduce anything new on race day." In other words, wear clothes in which you have trained, particularly shoes and socks. Of his many JFK starts, Storm failed to finish only two: his first attempt and a race in the late 1980s. The weather was bitterly cold, yet it was not to blame for his failure to reach Dam 4. What was the culprit? New socks. What had seemed like a good idea—purchasing socks with reinforced heels and toes—became Storm's undoing on the towpath as the extra material did not leave enough room in the shoes for his toes. *Do not introduce anything new . . .*

NUTRITION

More crucial than gear decisions, the seasoned ultrarunner plans for race-day nutrition—a vital component that the beginner tends to overlook or underestimate. For his first race, Storm carried a leather pouch that held candy and a cup for water on the towpath; now he prepares protein drinks and takes baby aspirin to help move lactic acid out of and nutrients in to his muscles. Downs "blew through" the aid stations during his first race, which meant he didn't get nutrients he sorely needed. "Around mile 27, I started getting horrible muscle cramps like my muscles were folding over themselves," Downs wrote. A lesson well-learned. For his second JFK, he was sure to eat plenty of food along the course.

Diets vary from runner to runner. Gowen drinks the vitamin- and nutrient-rich Ensure. Will Brown's report on JFK 1996 included this note, "I stayed well hydrated, and the electrolyte tabs, rock salt, and IB that I took probably contributed to a strong finish." The race menu selected by the Grimm guys seems unconventional, but it served the purpose of fueling their bodies: yogurt and PBJ sandwiches at Weverton, chicken noodle soup at Antietam, and Burger King vanilla milkshakes at Shepherdstown.

RACE DAY STRATEGY

Practical matters aside, a JFK runner quickly learns that the race is more than a physical test: it's a brain game. Here, the veteran has a distinct advantage, since knowing the terrain is essential in developing an effective race-day plan of action. The terrain, course configuration, positioning of aid stations—all of these elements figure into a runner's overall strategy. Because success is tied so closely to the nature of the course, strategy notes have been included in the next chapter, The Course.

A New Perspective

by Alan Gowen

Alan and Pam Gowen

JFK 2007 was to be my 62nd ultra. It was to be my 23rd consecutive month in which I'd completed an ultramarathon. It was to be my 11th ultra of the year having already completed two forty-milers, one 50-miler, one hundred-miler and six 50-kilometer races. I was in the best running shape of my life, and even at age 57 this year I'd run 5 PRs. I'd already planned on going for what I believed to be an easily obtainable PR in my 9th JFK.

You know though what they say about the best laid plans. Labor Day weekend brought a spectacular 27.5-mile run for fun on the brutally rugged Tuscarora Trail on Saturday, a 50-mile bike ride on Sunday, and a temporary end to my running and all my running plans when I tore my hamstring while playing tennis with Pam on Monday.

This was a tough blow for me for many reasons but particularly because of what JFK means. I have trouble articulating exactly what JFK is all about, but suffice it to say that despite finishing so many races—some of which are longer and more difficult—JFK remains the big one. It is so different from any other ultra I've ever experienced. JFK is a journey. JFK is the sunlight just peeking over South Mountain as you climb uphill at the start, and the sun going down as you slog along those final miles on those small country lanes, air turning cooler in those final miles. It's all those huge Sycamores on the other side of the river shining brilliant white in the late day sun. It's those aid stations where hundreds cheer you on, everyone a hero. JFK is eleven hundred everymen moving, some fast, some slow, and many in the middle; a conga line that stretches 50 miles from dawn to darkness. It's the lights of Downsville coming on as you pass through. JFK is a journey. It's moving from one town to another and taking all day to do it. It's Boonsboro just waking up and Williamsport just shutting down.

As race day approached I had some moments of hope for my recovery, but ultimately I knew that in 2007 it was my destiny to be on the sidelines at JFK, crewing for Pam. Pam had been having a good year running and had been training very hard for several months which had already yielded some amazing results and several PRs for her, too. There was no doubt that her 7th JFK was going to be her fastest by a good margin, and I was glad I'd have the chance to help her along the way.

And then in a heartbeat, those plans were gone, too. Pam's doctor ordered her to stop running—at least for the short term. Suddenly, after planning for months, our calendar for November 17 was disappointingly empty.

A New Perspective *(continued)*

What to do? Let's go anyway! We had dozens of friends who were going to be running, and we decided to spend the day cheering them on. Just as sure as turkeys and Pilgrims in November, if it's the Saturday before Thanksgiving, Boonsboro is where we're supposed to be. We just couldn't stay away.

We timed our arrival at the Weverton aid station so that we'd be able to see our friends Anstr Davidson and his ex-wife Lucia as they came through. Anstr was running his 25th consecutive JFK, and I was planning to spend a short time running with him later in the day. Anstr and Lucia were just coming through when we arrived, and after cheering them on we spent another couple of hours greeting runners as they arrived at the aid station. On the Saturday before Thanksgiving in 1996, as I toed the line for my first JFK, except for Pam and my daughter who were there with me, I didn't know any other person in Boonsboro.

Now, as Pam and I stood there at Weverton, we must have greeted over 200 runners whom we either recognized from this and all the other ultras we've run or considered some of our closer friends we've made through running. And it all began at JFK 11 years before. Fraternity, brotherhood, family—call it what you will, it was humbling for Pam and me as we stood there to feel the full impact of what this annual event has brought to us on a personal level.

Different runners had different styles as they came through the aid station. Lloyd was obviously on a mission. Paul was very methodical. And Dave and Kevin were clearly focused on their goal as they came running in, identical twins, on a perfect 10-hour pace.

We left Weverton and made our way to Antietam. The enormity of this event is lost on the runners. From the runner's perspective, it's all about the towpath—that tunnel through the trees. The runners have no idea of the hundreds of cars, thousands of supporters, police, fire and EMT personnel, rangers, and who knows what else, constantly on the move as a huge migration of humanity makes its way; the mammoth circus moving from town to town, aid station to aid station across the countryside.

At Antietam we once again saw Dave and Kevin running with the precision of a machine. Running as one, maintaining that perfect 10-hour pace. When Anstr arrived, I fell in with him and his 25th consecutive finish entourage and ran slowly along, feeling now somehow a part of the spectacle. At Shepherdstown I had to wait only a short time before Lloyd came running into view. I ran with him, as he made his way farther along into the great adventure.

Lloyd was very focused and moving at a great pace. During our time together he mentioned he didn't know exactly how he was doing, but I told him he was doing well and made a note to have some split information for him later. We saw Mike off and on. Although he was on a good pace, it was obvious he wasn't having the type of day he had hoped for. All along the way I had the opportunity to greet friends and running buddies as we made our way, step by step, closer and closer, while this tide of humanity rolled on, unstoppable, toward its destiny.

I left Lloyd to his step counting at Snyder's Landing. Pam and I moved on to Taylor's Landing, and when Lloyd came running through I let him know that he was only about 5 minutes off of a 10-hour pace. We kept getting glimpses of the Dave and Kevin machine, rhythmically moving in perfect unison, never missing a beat. We were enjoying ourselves enormously, caught up in the spectacle of JFK.

We hung out in Downsville, and when Anstr and Lucia arrived, Pam fell in with them. Last year Pam had run just about all of JFK with Anstr and Lucia, until she pulled away at the end, and so joining them for their final four miles was special for all of them.

I made my way to the middle school, parked the car, and began walking back out on the course, greeting runners I knew as they came into view. The first two coming strongly toward the finish were Dave and Kevin; high fives for these guys, getting it done in an amazing 9:56. When I got almost to the one-mile-to-go marker, I saw Lloyd approaching. I turned around and ran with him. His pace was constant all day long, and now it was no different. He made his way methodically over the last part of the course, running hard up the final hill to the cheers of everyone as he crossed the finish line—another great JFK under his belt.

Just before we reached the finish line, I peeled off from Lloyd and began once again making my way backward on the course, congratulating the runners I passed until, at just a little bit over a half mile from the finish, Pam came running into view with Anstr, Lucia and the 25th consecutive JFK finish entourage. I joined in and jogged the final stretch with them as they finished to the cheers of the crowd.

We hung out at the finish line, and we hung out in the gym. We congratulated Paul on his remarkable 26th consecutive finish. We talked and visited with many of the friends we'd seen only briefly as they ran past us during the day.

From a runner's point of view, JFK is an individual experience. It's the runner against the course or the clock. It's about determination and will. It's about limitations or exceeding expectations. Just the runner and his thoughts, one foot in front of the other, daylight shifting and time passing. But for Pam and me, this year brought us a different experience. We felt in some small way we were actually part of the race when we got to jog along with friends and encourage others who passed by. We were there with literally hundreds of our friends who knew exactly how we felt. We experienced JFK on an entirely different level; ants in a line making their way up the canal. Runners, supporters, crews and massive humanity stretched across 50 miles moving steadily toward Williamsport, a tide washing along, the enormity of the whole masking the individuality of the participants, the tail of the beast slowly getting shorter, as the giant finally began to obtain its victories.

We were here and we were there. It seemed we were everywhere. We had all of the fun, all of the experience and all of the joy of race day without any of the suffering. If we couldn't run, this is as good as it could possibly be. Sharing this with so many others was an experience we never would have had if things had gone as we'd originally planned. We'll always be thankful for being able to share as we did and for gaining a completely new perspective on this race that's so special to both of us.

Photo by Brenda Davidson

ONCE IS NOT ENOUGH. #727 Kevin Sayers at Crampton Gap during JFK 2005. Sayers is known for running in 1998 a "double JFK" with Tom Green. Starting the night before at the finish line in Williamsport, the duo ran the course in reverse to the starting line in Boonsboro then turned around and retraced their steps. Sayers completed the official JFK 1998—the second half of his 100-mile challenge—in 11:22:36.

The Course

JFK 50 MILE

START	LOCATION	TERRAIN
Mile 0	**BOONSBORO** Downtown on US 40 Alt	Paved road is flat for about 1 mile, then climbs uphill 500 feet to the Appalachian Trail
2.6	**APPALACHIAN TRAIL** Checkpoint #1 Reno Monument	Rocky trail of North-South footpath with demanding ups and downs and a series of steep switchbacks at mile 14.5
15.5	**WEVERTON** Checkpoint #2	Switchbacks end at paved road. Course returns to footpath east of Route 340, crosses railroad tracks and reaches C & O canal at mile marker 58.
22.4	**DARGAN** Checkpoint #3 *Halfway point*	Hard-packed dirt of the C & O Canal towpath, the flattest portion of the course through mile 41.8. Potomac River on left; canal on right
27.1	**ANTIETAM** Checkpoint #4	Flat, hard-packed dirt.
38.4	**TAYLOR'S LANDING** Checkpoint #5	Flat, hard-packed dirt until end of towpath at mile marker 84.
41.8	**DAM 4** Checkpoint #6	Paved road. Steep hill off of towpath for 1/3 mile; rolling paved roads for remaining 8.4 miles.
46.0	**DOWNSVILLE** Checkpoint #7	Paved road. This can be the coldest portion of the race when many run under the cover of darkness.
50.2 FINISH	**WILLIAMSPORT** Springfield Middle School	

COURSE AT A GLANCE

STRATEGY / NOTES	CUTOFF, 7 AM START
Check the impulse to surge ahead of the pack.	**7 AM** official start *5 AM alternate*
Pay attention to footing. Avoid sharp rocks. Many walk up the steep paved road from Reno Monument Road to Lamb's Knoll, the course high point.	**9:30 AM** at Gathland Gap, 9.3 miles
Safely avoid being caught by the train which can add minutes to total race time.	**11:30 AM** at Weverton Aid Station

Overcome boredom. Scenery is beautiful, but monotonous. Leg strength while jogging indicates how smoothly next half of race will go.	
Many racers report their endurance and commitment is tested at the 30-mile point, past Shepherdstown Bridge.	**1:45** at Antietam Aid Station **3 PM** at Snyder's Landing, 34.4 miles **4 PM** at Taylor's Landing

Run to the finish. Some benefit from changing to a lightweight racing flat; others need the ankle support of a heavier shoe.	**5 PM** at Dam 4
If unable to run to the finish, work the terrain: walk uphill, jog down. Keep moving.	**6 PM** at Downsville
Enjoy the thrill of reaching the finish line.	**7 PM** Runners must exit course for safety reasons.

The JFK 50 Mile draws a backward J across the county map below Hagerstown. From the starting line in Boonsboro, runners climb to the top of South Mountain, then wind downward to the Potomac River and finish in low-lying Williamsport. Along this course, they encounter three distinct types of terrain which lend the race its unique character: the trail, the towpath, and the pavement. This progression from rocky to smooth surface works in favor of the runners as they tire. The sections, however, are not equally portioned, as more than half of the course takes place on 26.3 miles of towpath—a marathon-length race within a race.

Interspersed along the course are more than a dozen aid stations, stocked with not only first aid supplies but also drinks and food. The stations serve double-duty as checkpoints or "splits," where runners' times are recorded. "There is a time limit for each check point," George Banker notes on the event Web site, "and you can be pulled off the course for not maintaining pace." Time limits are a safety measure that also guarantee runners meet the National Park Service requirement to exit the towpath by dusk. The 2008 race application specifies these limits:

MILE	LOCATION	CUTOFF PER START TIME 7 AM	5 AM	
9.3	Gathland Gap	9:30 AM	8:30 AM	
15.5	Weverton	11:30 AM	10:30 AM	
27.1	Antietam	1:45 PM	1:00 PM	*Halfway point*
34.5	Snyder's Landing	3:00 PM	2:45 PM	
38.4	Taylor's Landing	4:00 PM	4:00 PM	
41.8	Dam # 4	5:00 PM	5:00 PM	*Exit towpath*
46.0	Downsville	6:00 PM	6:00 PM	
50.2	Williamsport	7:00 PM	7:00 PM	

Although more time is allocated for pre-dawn starters to reach the early checkpoints, everyone must arrive at Taylor's Landing no later than 4 PM.

Pacing is key, whether one's goal is to finish in a top spot or simply to finish. Clifton set the course record by maintaining an average pace of 6:56 minutes per mile. A typical participant covers a mile in about 12 minutes—faster along smooth surfaces, more slowly on the Appalachian Trail and as the race wears on. In order to log 50 miles in the allotted time, the average pace can not fall below 14:24 for 7 AM starters or 16:48 for pre-dawn starters.

Strategy: Pacing

JFK veterans know precisely the time they should reach each checkpoint in order to stay on track. This information helps a runner to gauge progress and to adjust pace accordingly. A typical runner expects the pace to be slow along the Appalachian Trail, pick up on the way to Dargan and Antietam, then slow again around Taylor's Landing where fatigue is apt to set in. One atypical runner in 2007 was Bryon Powell who continually improved his pace from start to finish. In his blog at irunfar.blogspot.com, Powell rated the JFK his best event that year, not just because he was on the winning men's team, but also because he gave the race all he had: "I started out strong, steadily increased my effort, never backed off—even for a couple minutes, and came into the finish spent." Powell's splits prove his point:

CHECKPOINT	POWELL'S PACE
Weverton	9:18
Dargan	9:02
Antietam	8:54
Taylor's Landing	8:45
Dam 4	8:44
Downsville	8:42
Finish	8:39

Compare this progression to the average pace for the top 100 finishers and to splits for the 2007 champion Michael Wardian. The top 100 numbers improve as expected until Taylor's Landing, where the tide turns. Like Powell, Wardian goes against the norm, distinguishing himself with a breakneck pace that actually improves at Taylor's Landing. Yet Wardian's pace begins to fall slightly by Downsville and toward the finish:

CHECKPOINT	POWELL	TOP 100	WINNER
Weverton	9:18	9:12	7:45
Dargan	9:02	8:55	7:25
Antietam	8:54	8:50	7:08
Taylor's Landing	8:45	8:54	6:53
Dam 4	8:44	8:56	6:52
Downsville	8:42	9:00	6:55
Finish	8:39	8:59	6:59

Although Powell's time to Weverton was slower than the top 100, his uncommon recovery enabled him to finish in 25th place (7:13:45).

[I] was on the starting line talking with Lloyd when the gun went off. At 7 a.m., with the sunrise just beginning to glow over South Mountain, we let the tide of 850 runners carry us along and into the day.

—Alan Gowen, JFK 2006

THE START

Three minutes before 7 AM on race day, downtown Boonsboro is thick with smiling people in brightly colored shirts and hats, their muscled legs exposed to the ankles, bouncing on the balls of their feet atop the asphalt. Noisy with excitement, they ignore the double yellow lines and fill both lanes of US 40 Alt. A rough rectangle about 15 people wide by 60 deep faces east.

The retort of a gun sounds, and their voices raise as one in a cheer. They're off, moving as a unit. No great hurry. This race will not be won by a quick start nor lost by a slow one. Many set their watches.

Slowly, the group expands. Stretching—stretching along the first flat mile. Then, during a steep uphill climb (shown at right), the bulk begin to separate. Those in front are careful not to break ahead too quickly, those in back cautious about falling too far behind.

Ascent to the Appalachian Trail

As the sun crosses the sky, the spread will lengthen to span 25 miles.

By the top of the mountain, the initial width of more than a dozen racers narrows significantly. The terrain demands it. At the Old South Mountain Inn, runners step off of the pavement and onto the Appalachian Trail.

Strategy: From the start to the trail

> **. . . what my Mom said was, I can't win on the trail, but I could definitely lose on the trail.**
> —Mackenzie Riford, *RunnersWorld*, 2007

To run or not to run? That is the question many have answered long before reaching downtown Boonsboro. Yet a runner who decides while training to conserve energy at the start can get caught up in the excitement of race day and throw caution to the wind. And pacing is not the only consideration; portions of the Appalachian Trail are narrow. David Grimm notes, "We don't want to go out too fast, but don't want to let too many slow people on the trail in front of us." Anstr Davidson also expressed this quandary:

> You run up Route 40 Alternate on a gentle hill to the AT trailhead. This road is runnable, but it increases your pulse rate. Do you run or walk? Your first of many hard decisions all day. Run and pay later, or walk and look like a wimp. Gain a few seconds, or allow people to pass you who will soon block your way on the trail. (2004)

Gowen wrestled with this dilemma in 2006 and had made up his mind to conserve energy not only at the start but also on the AT. That way, when he reached the towpath he would have the energy to run well. A sound plan, though he did not carry it out and paid the price later in the race:

> . . . It took less than a quarter mile for me to be overcome by adrenaline, enthusiasm, excitement and just plain stupidity and abandon my carefully crafted plan. I felt great and I just tried to stay in the moment, have fun, and let the course dictate how hard I pushed. I covered the first 9 miles faster than ever before (Slow Down! I told myself), and I was through the 16 miles of Appalachian Trail in three hours, again faster than ever before. As I made my turn onto the towpath, I felt OK but was already regretting my early stupid enthusiasm.
>
> As I moved along up the towpath, I seemed to be holding a good pace, but I felt a lot more fatigued than was comfortable for this point in the race. . . .

Storm also takes it easy in the early hours but realizes he could get trapped behind slow movers on the AT:

> Cresting the first hill a bit east of Boonsboro's heart, I notice the leaders have already turned this tide into a monstrous mass of silly putty stretching clear over and past Route 67. My strategy is to conserve energy . . . not get caught up in this abundance of exuberance surrounding me. The downside of this plan is it will put me behind those who, after expending so much energy covering the five miles uphill to Lambs Knoll, become super cautious, slowly picking their way over . . . every rock in their path.

7 AM STARTERS MUST REACH				
MILE	BY	IN	DISTANCE	MIN. PACE
9.3 Gathland Gap	9:30 AM	2.5 HRS	9.3 MI	16:07
15.5 Weverton	11:30 AM	2.0 HRS	6.2 MI	19:21

THE TRAIL

Runners follow an alternate North–South footpath, a rocky and challenging trek that begins west of the official AT and meanders on to and off of the trail. This route is better-suited for race purposes, as it is more of a straight shot to Lamb's Knoll and includes a 1-1/2-mile stretch of paved road—a well-earned respite from trail hazards.

Running atop the mountain ridge, mindful of sharp rocks and tree roots, a runner must watch his step. Though the footwork demands concentration, this portion of the course is, for many, the favorite. Since the race has barely begun, excitement and energy remain high. The scenery is beautiful, and the rising sun filters between the trees making patterns of light and shadows on the path. Leaves crunch underfoot. The passage is anything but boring.

One break in the footpath takes place at Reno Monument Road, where runners land on a paved, one-lane stretch of nearly two miles. The smooth surface would be a welcome respite from the trail's hazards, if not for the steep incline that leads to Lamb's Knoll. This is the course highpoint, and most conserve energy by walking, not running, the 1.9 miles to its peak.

After Lamb's Knoll, the trail picks up and follows many ups and downs en route to Gathland State Park. Just before the park, another break in the footpath is preempted by a difficult area that is side-turned and narrow, strewn with rocks and tree roots. Sometimes referred to as a dirt toboggan slide, this natural impediment empties into the park beside the ruins of a late-19th-century barn.

View from the bottom of the hill toward Lamb's Knoll—the course high point.

The brief interlude across Gathland park is the calm before the storm, as the next leg of the trail leads to Weverton Cliffs. The rocky downhill passes along the way warrant caution, yet at least one runner employs a risky technique to traverse these areas:

> This is the same point I like to take advantage of the speed increase presented by downhill rock hopping, saving valuable time . . . although it could come at a price if I'm not careful. For if nothing else this trail is famous for an abundance of rock traps which lurk beneath fall's carpet of leaves . . . [this is] the most enjoyable part of today: flying over broken ground. (Storm, 2007)

In the last half mile before the cliffs, patches of bare earth suitable for placing feet become scarce, exacting a toll on each runner. The course veers west before the cliffs, following instead a series of switchbacks that are usually described as treacherous.

Many believe that the first off Weverton cliffs can not win the JFK 50 Mile. If this were true, you might say Michael Wardian's first-place finish in 2007 was saved when Zachariah Miller and Eric Grossman landed in Weverton ahead of the pack, 3 minutes shy of 2 hours. Wardian reached the checkpoint

The "dirt toboggan slide" at right leads into Gathland State Park beside the ruins of a barn, below.

A welcome end to the switchbacks.

at 9 AM sharp with an elite group of eight other thirty-somethings, including JFK 2006 champion Pete Breckinridge; Canadian Eric Deshaies; and top 10 finishers Matthew Lavine, Mark Lundblad, Blake Benke, Greig Arendt, Ian Torrence and Gregory Crowther. The next group did not hit Weverton for seven more minutes.

A superstitious runner might hesitate to arrive in Weverton first, but should not hold back from being among the first. All but three of the eleven runners mentioned above went on to finish in the top 10 of JFK 2007. Miller came in second.

In fact, the first to Weverton can win the race. In 2003, Dave Mackey and Clark Zealand reached the Weverton checkpoint first at 1:55, and Mackey went on to win the event. (Coincidentally, Miller and Grossman placed 2nd and 3rd that year.) Other JFK champions who also led the group into Weverton include Paul South in 2004 and Courtney Campbell in 1999.

On the flip side, a slower pace on the Appalachian Trail does not rule out a top finish. Although Andrew Mason reached Weverton a full 23 minutes after Miller and Grossman in 2007, Mason improved his pace on the towpath and pavement to achieve a ninth-place finish.

Despite the sharp rocks, unexpected dips and steep inclines, the trail portion of the JFK 50 Mile has a low attrition rate. Of the 1,198 starters in 2007, for example, only 8 runners failed to reach the next stop at Dargan.

Crossing the tracks without being delayed by a train is a stroke of good fortune. The marathon-length towpath lurks a few paces beyond.

In 22 years, I have only been caught by the train one time. But each year, it catches someone. This year, as I descend into Weverton, I hear the train's horn blaring . . .

—Anstr Davidson

THE TOWPATH

Navigating the trail and surviving the switchbacks qualifies a runner for the marathon that starts at C&O Canal mile marker 58. One step onto the towpath begins the longest and flattest portion of the ultra—a 26-mile stretch that is the antithesis of the Appalachian Trail.

Jogging on the hard-packed surface, a runner is freed from focusing on footwork and able to take stock. What time is it? Am I behind goal? On track? How do my legs feel? Can I continue at this pace?

Heading upstream, tracing the Maryland border beneath a canopy of trees, a runner's view to the left is the Potomac River and Sycamore trees growing along its West Virginia bank. Energy starts to wane. Muscles tire. Accompanying fatigue is boredom. Ten miles pass. Fifteen. The body weakens, while the scenery remains constant: canopy of trees, river flowing past, Sycamore trees in the distance.

> **Because the event is half physical and half mental toughness, it's been said the JFK doesn't really begin until after the Shepherdstown Bridge.**
>
> —Lloyd Storm

At this point in the race, the attrition rate begins to climb. In 2007, another 55 dropped out before Taylor's Landing. The 30-mile mark is a turning point, where the body is apt to rebel against the beating it has been taking and the mind must fight an enemy worse than boredom: Negativity. "I could stop. Look! There's my handler. Do I really *need* to finish?" Many runners recount 30-mile horror stories in which their determination to reach Williamsport is sorely tested.

Passing the 30-mile barrier, however, puts a runner over the hump. Progressing this far means the mental battle waged on the towpath has been won. After the Taylor's Landing checkpoint in 2007, only 14 called it quits. The remainder carried on to hear the water spilling over Dam 4, announcing the end of the waterside marathon, carried on to take that final step off of the towpath and onto the pavement to begin the home stretch.

Is #121 Renee Butler smiling for the camera or just happy to reach the Antietam Checkpoint during JFK 2005? Butler, 44, of Bethesda, Md., finished in 8:52:58. Also visible are #655 Brian Hendricks, 33, of Bethlehem, Pa., (8:45:16) and #1238 Cameron Campbell.

MILE	7 AM STARTERS MUST REACH			
	BY	IN	DISTANCE	MIN. PACE
27.1 Antietam	1:45 PM	2.25 HRS	11.6 MI	11:38
34.5 Snyder's Lndg	3:00 PM	2.75 HRS	7.4 MI	22:18
38.4 Taylor's Lndg	4:00 PM	1.00 HRS	3.9 MI	15:24
41.8 Dam # 4	5:00 PM	1.00 HRS	3.4 MI	17:36

Strategy: Finding the run–walk ratio

On the towpath, the dilemma over whether or not to run changes to "What should my run–walk ratio be?" The correct proportion is runner-specific, and the individual variations can make for amusing moments, as James Kahler noted during JFK 2007:

> Many people started into their run/walk right from the beginning of the C & O portion. It was kind of funny. I'd get passed, see them stop a couple hundred yards up and then I run by them. I'd get passed and then see them stop. Picture this repeating for 30 miles.

Photo by Brenda Davidson

Chatting along the towpath near Antietam during JFK 2006 are #1011 Anstr Davidson and #826 Terry Hawk, 48, of Concord, Ohio, who finished 91st in 8:14:23.

Dam 4 signals the end of the towpath's beauty—and monotony. Once runners cross through the canal bed, the sound of rushing water recedes beneath a muffled cadence of rubber soles on blacktop.

Grimm aimed to run for four minutes and walk for one, but knew this would fluctuate on race day. At the first aid station, his son wanted to switch to 3–2 intervals and Grimm reluctantly agreed.

Gowen's strategy on the towpath is to check his progress every few miles. While running alongside the Potomac River, he mentally calculates his pace and decides whether it must be maintained or increased in order to meet his set time limit.

Not all runners have the timing worked out in advance. Will Brown of Raleigh, N.C., came across another runner on the towpath whose pacing seemed to match his own:

> A guy named Don Clark from St. Paul, MN, was my saviour. We had been hopscotching each other for a few miles, and I fell into his pacing routine. I asked him what it was, and he grinned and said it was "Run when you can, walk when you can't." I asked if he would mind if I fell in behind him and did what he did. . . . We discovered we had both run the Bull Run Run 50 miler back in the spring. I stayed with him to the end of the Towpath, and we parted company at the 41.9 mile aid station there. (1996)

Brown finished in 10:25:32, not far ahead of his towpath companion, Clark (10:39:48).

Those who find a comfortable run–walk pattern might reach the Antietam checkpoint ready to take on whatever suprises the second half of the course holds in store. Here, a JFK veteran can be a good companion for a first-timer to have, as Grimm notes, "I warned Kevin not to get too excited, because we all know that from Sheperdstown to Dam 4 is a physical and mental test."

The last six miles are the hardest in a marathon. Contrary, the last six miles of a 50-miler are comparatively easier. You've already run 44—what's six more?

—Vic Culp, JFK 1996

THE PAVEMENT

No other point on the JFK 50 Mile, short of the finish line, offers more positive reinforcement than the pavement at mile 41.8. The sight of that narrow strip of blacktop is an immediate pick-me-up that can dramatically improve a runner's mental outlook. By now, two races have been completed successfully: an extreme trail plus a marathon. The pavement is the crowning glory of the terrain triad.

Although they take to the changed surface with renewed optimism—*just 8.4 miles to go!*—veterans know what to expect. First-timers, however, are in jeopardy of having their enthusiasm squelched. Around the first bend, is the steepest hill since Lamb's Knoll, many hours ago.

The C & O marathon exit ramp

Most overcome this obstacle at a walk, commencing a walk–jog pattern that varies with the terrain—walk uphill, jog down . . . walk uphill, jog down. Gone is the concentration on footwork, fading is the concern for time as all is overshadowed by the need to keep pressing forward. Passing farms and animals in the fields, walking and jogging along the rolling country roads, a runner might wonder if the race will ever end.

Farther down the road, closer to Downsville and Williamsport, traffic is apt to be a factor.

The sun moves closer to the western horizon. Daylight wanes.

On the bright side, a runner who conquers the hill beyond Dam 4 is likely to reach the finish. In JFK 2007, only one percent of the starting lineup dropped out along the paved roads between Dam 4 and Williamsport.

Strategy: Keep moving

Elite runners see the blacktop as their cue to run full out to a strong finish. Others expect to continue a run–walk pattern with one essential alteration: Stop working the clock and start working the terrain. Walk uphill, run down. Should this approach fail due to unforeseen circumstances, runners move forward as best as they are able: *Run when you can, walk when you can't.*

While logging those training miles equivalent to a trip to the Rockies, a runner has ample time to decide how to deal with this last portion of the course. Yet the best laid plans can be left behind in the towpath's dust, so that strategy must be formulated in the heat of the moment. Here, runners take stock and make late-in-the-race adjustments to their game plans.

The pavement is the bottom of the ninth, the score is 4–5 and the bases are loaded. Do you bunt and tie the game? Or go for the win—hit it out of the park and exit the field on your teammate's shoulders?

The pavement is the third down, the score is 21–24, and the clock shows less than a minute left. Do you punt and go into overtime? Or run the ball into the end zone while the crowd goes wild?

The pavement is a quick mental calculation. If I maintain pace, will I reach my goal? The answer depends on one's definition of a win. An elite runner vieing for first place is likely to answer no, since a successful finish depends on giving it all he's got. This runner goes for the trip to home plate, the drive for the end zone. For the majority, however, the answer hinges on how the race has progressed thus far. Yes, a runner can maintain pace if it enables her to reach Springfield Middle School within her personal time goal. Success can be achieved with a bunt or field goal.

And what if the mental calculation reveals numbers that are not favorable? The Grimms aimed to complete the race in less than 10 hours. At mile 42, David did the math and found they were about four minutes too slow. He told his son it was time to make a decision. They could coast in or "make a run for it" and try to meet their self-imposed 10-hour limit. A long year of training influenced Kevin's response: "Let's go!" By Downsville, the pair were back on track.

Gowen was similarly disappointed by the numbers once he hit the pavement in 2006:

> At the 42-mile point, as I turned off the towpath and onto those final 8.2 miles of rolling country roads that lead to the finish, I checked my chart again and saw that if I slowed down at all I would finish over 10 hours. . . . I dug down once more and turned it up a very small notch.

But a few miles later, his body rebelled against the punishment. Fighting severe cramps in his right hamstring, Gowen felt his 10-hour finish "slipping away one more time." A couple of miles before Springfield Middle School, he saw in the distance his wife Pam, who had started at 5 a.m. Continuing to fight the cramps by stopping and stretching from time to time, Gowen finally gained on his wife at mile 49. "Pam and I were now, for the first time ever in an ultra, running together." Hand-in-hand they crossed the finish. Determination won out, as Gowen achieved his second best JFK time of 9:52:45.

Downs, too, paid for his decision to go for the goal in 2007 with pain along the pavement:

> My experience from the year before had given me wisdom, and I avoided getting any injuries. I paced myself much slower with more rests, and ate plenty of food along the way. Unfortunately, I was pacing myself a little too slow. When I got to the "8 miles to go" mark, I looked at my watch and saw that I had a little over an hour to do all 8 remaining miles to beat my goal time. . . I was averaging 11 min per mile . . . I took off, refusing to slow down even though the pain was nearly driving me to tears. The announcer's voice rang over the cheering crowd, "and here comes a young one, Alan Downs, 19, from Clear Spring." I raced the clock and crossed the finish line, beating my goal by several minutes.

7 AM STARTERS MUST REACH

MILE		BY	IN	DISTANCE	MIN. PACE
46.0	Downsville	6:00 PM	1 HR	4.2 MI	14.3
50.2	Finish Line	7:00 PM	1 HR	4.2 MI	14.3

> By mile 47, I know I'm going to finish.
> It's hard to hold back a tear or two.
>
> —Vic Culp, JFK 1996

THE FINISH

Suddenly, the race does end. At the tip of the course's backward J in Williamsport, runners crest the last small hill and see ahead and to the left the red brick façade of Springfield Middle School.

The crowd cheers.

Grimm remembers, "Coming up the final stretch, we paused for one last walk—so that we could run it in." He had planned to hang back and give his son bragging rights, but Kevin insisted they finish side-by-side. Gowen appeared from the crowd to give David a high five. The finish line was one step ahead; then one step behind. "At 9:56:08, we reached our year-long goal," Grimm said.

How different the scene from sunrise to sunset: fifty miles has changed the densely packed group, bouncing and chattering with anticipation, into a scattering of individuals, zapped of strength. Their vitality having been emptied along the beautiful mountaintop trail, the serene riverside towpath, and the pastoral paved roads, runners slow to a stop, collapse on the lawn, fall into the arms of a loved one.

The goal at 7 AM was lofty: complete an ultramarathon. The goals at 7 PM are more basic: Take a shower. Eat dinner. Sleep.

During the day, feelings shift from exhilaration to exhaustion. The temporary thrill of entering an ultramarathon is temporarily replaced by the exhaustion of running 50 miles and permanently replaced by the quiet and sustained satisfaction of crossing the finish.

Michael Wardian, the 2007 champion, approached his finish pointing to the sky to indicate his number one status. According to Banker's article at JFK50mile.org, Wardian credited his win in part to a well-executed race strategy: "I think my fitness level and patience early in the race paid off for me at JFK. Also, I feel like I finally ran a race where everything I have learned over the years came together and I executed my race strategy as thoroughly as possible."

After wrapping up a year of training by running 50 miles, a runner finds gestures easier to come by than words. At the finish line, the JFK 50-miler slaps a high five, revels in a victory hug, points to the sky.

Michael Wardian, champion, JFK 2007

Despite all the success I've found this year . . . The JFK 50 Mile still remains The Big One. . . . It's the one that got me running. It's the one that changed my life. It's the one that holds that magic spell.

—Alan Gowen, JFK 2006

Fifty Years

Approaching a Milestone

No anniversary could be more important in the history of the JFK 50 Mile than the one to be celebrated in November 2012. It's the golden one—the 50th—when the event that promotes endurance will achieve matching longevity, marking one event for each course mile.

A 50-year streak.

Who will gather in downtown Boonsboro to celebrate this milestone? The usual suspects, whose names are recorded in the annals displayed at JFK50mile.org, plus about one-third newcomers.

We can predict that the bulk of the group will be race veterans, because the race is addictive. You can't run just one. The trail–towpath–pavement symphony calls like a siren. Like a song stuck in your head. It's catchy.

During the last half-century, the race has accumulated a dedicated following. For those who do not enter other ultramarathons, the JFK 50 Mile can assume a grand stature. In their lives, the race is more than an event; it's a lifestyle. Training becomes an integral part of daily schedules, orchestrating choices about what to eat, when to sleep, and how to spend free time.

Stopping can be difficult.

Particularly when you consider the streak.

Crossing the finish line first is not the only way to make JFK 50 Mile history. In the same way that baseball honors Cal Ripken, who was not the number-one hitter but who was a consistent and persistent player, the JFK ultra recognizes its iron-men and -women. Individuals who have completed the JFK course 10 years in a row are called "streakers." Those completing five or more events—consecutive or not—achieve membership in mileage clubs, starting with the 250-Mile Club and continuing in 250-mile increments to the prestigious 1,500-Mile Club. The clubs as well as the streaker designation motivate runners who might otherwise take a year off. Membership reinforces the fact that ultramarathons are races defined by more than speed. An ultramarathon is above all else a celebration of individual endurance.

> **JFK is more like a demanding religion. You don't love it, but you are dedicated to it. I don't love being in Boonsboro every November; I just have to be.**
> —Anstr Davidson

Storm, for example, is a streaker, having finished 13 back-to-back JFK 50 Mile runs. His desire to continue the streak dissuades him from taking a year off. He is also a member of the 750-Mile Club, qualified by finishing at least 15 events. By completing 19 total events, he needs just one more for admittance to the 1,000-Mile Club. After JFK 2005, this club counted only 15 members, including Paul Betker and Anstr Davidson. More scarce is membership in the 1,250-Mile Club which had 8 members in 2005 and in the 1,500-Mile Club which had only four members. The longest streak of consecutive finishes is 37, achieved by Kim Byron, who logged a total 1,850 JFK race miles.

Anstr Davidson admits that the streak is a motivator, but finds his commitment to the event runs deeper than any honorary designation:

> Sure the streak keeps me going, but the real reason I want to come back to JFK is that it has become part of the yearly cycle of my life. JFK marks the beginning of the holiday season. It is as much a part of the calendar as Thanksgiving, Christmas, and New Year. It is a unifying force in my life. So many things have happened since I ran my first JFK in 1983. No matter what, JFK has always been there each November.

Ultra runners by definition are motivated. Goal-oriented. They think in the long-term. Though it is unlikely that in 1963 Buzz Sawyer would have entertained the notion of his event continuing for half of a century, the anniversary is not surprising in retrospect, when you consider the mentality of a super-long-distance runner. Upon crossing the finish line, before the wave of victory subsides, the JFK runner is apt to plan for the next year: What can I do differently to improve my time? Fatigued and breathless, runners leave Springfield Middle School, asking each other the inevitable question, "See you next year?" Responses run the gamut from an easy yes to a conflicted no.

The 46th annual JFK 50 Mile Run will take place on Saturday, November 22, 2008. The sun will rise at 7:03 a.m. and set at 4:51, leaving 1,000 runners nine hours and 48 minutes of daylight. Again relating the event history to the course, JFK 2008 is Downsville, with 4 more years to the finish.

Eight-year-old Doug Sease is shown on page 55 enjoying his first run on the rocky footpath near Old South Mountain Inn. By 2012, he will meet the race's minimum age requirement. Will Doug at 13 hit the street in Boonsboro the Saturday before Thanksgiving along with his grandfather, who is a race veteran?

Will anyone ever achieve a 50-year streak? Perhaps that victory is reserved for the king of ultramarathons. The JFK 50 Mile is the oldest and the largest 50-miler in America with historical roots and a course characterized by national landmarks. Its dedicated race directors and empassioned runners return year after year to put one foot in front of the other more times than one can count to cover 50 miles.

See You Next Year?

Yes, I'll be there. If I can't run, I'll walk. —Lloyd Storm

Now a fearless two-time veteran of the 50-miler, I am resting up for the next long run. —Alan Downs

Maybe. I was thinking of coming back to JFK next year as a walk. Do your legs still ache when you take 13 hours rather than 8? —Vic Culp

That's it. I'm done. Officially retired . . . I'm not even thinking that I've finished seven and three more makes ten and the 500-Mile Club. Or that with a little more training I might be able to set a PR before I'm too old . . .
 —David Grimm

JFK 2000 photo by Bunny Runyan

Resources

Banker, George (2007). "Wardian's Third Time Is a Charm at JFK 50." Retrieved December 22, 2007, from www.JFK50mile.org.

Brown, Will (1996). JFK 50 Mile report to The Wired Running Club, Mid-Atlantic Dead Runners Society. Retrieved January 3, 2008, from www.geocities.com/madeads/will_jfk.html

Culp, Vic (1996). JFK 50 Mile report, Mid-Atlantic Dead Runners Society. Retrieved January 3, 2008, from www.geocities.com/madeads/vic_jfk.html

CVAC. Cumberland Valley Athletic Club's 2007 event program and 2008 pre-race packet.

Davidson, Anstr (2004). "Reflections on the JFK 50 Mile Run." Virginia Happy Trails Running Club. Retrieved December 23, 2007, from www.vhtrc.org/forum/jfk2004-ad.htm and eMails to author. Also see vhtrc.org for more photos of the race, like the one on p. 59.

Downs, Alan (2007). JFK 50 Mile report.

Frederick News-Post, Frederick, Md. (November 11, 2007). "Going the Distance—Riford, a 13-year-old, ready for JFK" by Karen Gardner. Retrieved December 30, 2007, from www.fredericknewspost.com/sections/archives

Gowen, Alan (2006, 2007). JFK 50 Mile reports.

Grimm, David (2007). JFK 50 Mile report.

Herald-Mail Company, Hagerstown, Md. Retrieved December 22, 2007, from the Herald-Mail.com:
- "Wardian posts 2nd-best time ever to comfortably win 45th JFK crown" by Chris Carter (November, 19, 2007).
- "Runnin' down a dream, mile by mile, year by year" by Andy Mason (November 2007).
- "He keeps in shape for the long run" by Janet Heim (December 12, 2002).

JFK50mile.org (2007). Official Web site of the JFK 50-Mile Run. Event and participant data, race history and links.

JFKlibrary.org (2008). Retrieved December 26, 2007, from the World Wide Web:

Robert F. Kennedy quote on p. 11.

Shape of Things to Come ad on p. 7 from "The Government Takes on Physical Fitness."

James Kahler (2007). "Tales from the Middle of the Pack," retrieved March 3, 2008, from jameskahler.com/recovering-from-50-miles

Bryon Powell (2007). Retrieved January 8, 2008, from Powell's blog at irunfar.blogspot.com. The site offers practical advice for newcomers in articles, such as "How to Select a First Ultramarathon" and "Training for Your First Ultramarathon."

President's Council on Physical Fitness and Sports (2006). "History of the President's Council on Physical Fitness and Sports (1956–2006)." 50th anniversary article retrieved December 23, 2007, from www.fitness.gov/50thanniversary/toolkit-firstfiftyyears.htm. The bulk of the text reprinted in the Appendix excludes quote outtakes and a list of members that appears at the end of the online article.

Planet Ultramarathon (October 10, 2007). "JFK 50 mile reaches new limit." Retrieved December 23, 2007, from www.planetultramarathon.wordpress.com/2007/10/10/jfk-50-mile-reaches-new-limit/

Runner's World (2007). Riford quote from video clip retrieved December 30, 2007, from www.RunnersWorld.com

Sayers, Kevin. "1998 JFK 50/100 Challenge Run Report." Retrieved August 30, 2008, from Kevin Sayers's UltRunR Web site at www.ultrunr.com/jfk100.html

Storm, Lloyd (2006, 2007). JFK 50 Mile reports and conversations with author.

Time magazine (1963).
Retrieved January 12, 2008, from www.Time.com/time/magazine/article
/0,9171,829887,00.html "Nip-Ups, Anyone?" (2/15/63)
/0,9171,827996,00.html "Hit the Road, Jack" (2/22/63)

Appendix

History of the President's Council on
Physical Fitness and Sports (1956–2006)

By the President's Council on Physical Fitness and Sports

In December 1953, Dr. Hans Kraus, M.D., associate professor of physical medicine and rehabilitation at New York University and an avid mountain climber, sounded an alarm. Kraus and his associate, Ms. Bonnie Prudden, published an article, "Muscular Fitness and Health," in the Journal of the American Association for Health, Physical Education, and Recreation, claiming that the nation was becoming soft. The affluent lifestyle of 20th century America was making life so easy and effortless that American adults and children were rapidly losing muscle tone. To compensate, the authors warned, Americans would have to engage in regular exercise to attain a state of physical fitness comparable to that of an earlier era, when Americans walked for transportation, worked on farms, and accomplished most activities of daily living and work through manual labor.

In the late 1940s and early 1950s, Kraus and his associates had published several other papers emphasizing the woeful state of the nation's physical fitness, including another article co-authored with Prudden (under the name Ruth P. Hirschland), which appeared in the New York State Journal of Medicine. Working with Dr. Sonja Weber at the Posture Clinic of Manhattan's Columbia–Presbyterian Hospital, Kraus had designed the Kraus–Weber Tests for Muscular Fitness. The article in the New York State Journal of Medicine reported the results of a study that administered the Kraus–Weber Tests to about 4,400 students between ages 6 and 16 in public school systems across the United States and to about 3,000 European students in the same age range in Switzerland, Italy, and Austria. The test results were startling: 56 percent of the U.S. students failed at least one of the test components, which included activities such as leg lifts, sit-ups, trunk lifts, and toe touches. However, only about 8 percent of the European children failed even one of the test components.

No matter what age, gender, or test, European kids held a decisive edge. Kraus attributed the test results to lifestyle. Europeans relied less on automobiles, school buses, and elevators. European children walked miles to school, rode bicycles, hiked, and chopped and hauled wood for home heating. In contrast, American children were largely driven in cars by their parents, confined to their own neighborhoods, and obligated to perform only easy chores such as making their own beds and setting the table, nothing more strenuous than walking the dog or mowing the lawn.

Kraus's article in the New York State Journal of Medicine caught the attention of John Kelly, a successful Philadelphia contractor better known as the father of actress Grace Kelly than as an athlete (national sculling champion) and wartime physical fitness officer. Horrified at the implications of Kraus's findings, Kelly passed the report along to Sen. James Duff of Pennsylvania. Duff was so shaken by Kraus's findings that he took the issue up with President Dwight D. Eisenhower, who reportedly stated that he too was "shocked" by the trends exposed by Kraus and called the test results "alarming."

In 1954, Kraus was invited to present his report to the national convention of the American Medical Association in Atlantic City. This opportunity gave him a forum to sound an alarm in the mainstream media. Magazines such as U.S. News and World Report, Newsweek, and Sports Illustrated seized on the test findings and provided interview opportunities for Kraus to put his messages front and center before the American people: Getting and maintaining physical fitness through exercise is key to physical and emotional well-being; U.S. children coming into the first grade were already muscle deficient; U.S. public schools weren't offering enough physical activity to reverse the trend.

The media "buzz" generated by Kraus, coupled with his determination to take his case to the highest levels of the federal government, finally began to get results. Despite lack of agreement among health and fitness professionals about the adequacy of the Kraus–Weber Tests and about the reliability of the results showing American children to be less fit than Europeans, many leaders in the physical education community viewed Kraus's work as a welcome opportunity to promote more school PE programs.

Kraus and Prudden were invited to a White House luncheon held on July 11, 1955, to present the findings of their report to 30 government leaders, medical researchers, and sports personalities. Following the luncheon, President Eisenhower directed Vice President Richard Nixon to call a meeting to decide what actions the government should take in view of Kraus's results. The resulting meeting took place less than a month later, on Aug. 8, 1955, and included Kraus and Prudden, sports leaders, government workers, and educators. That group, in turn, recommended that the focus of the government response should be youth fitness and called for a conference of leaders and experts to develop specific recommendations.

Although the conference was scheduled to be held immediately, it was delayed almost a year because of the president's illness. Finally, on June 18–19, 1956, the President's Conference on the Fitness of American Youth was held at the United States Naval Academy in Annapolis, Md. At the president's direction, Nixon presided as conference chairman. Attending were 140 participants, including Kraus and Prudden; national, state, and local government leaders; educators; people representing the fields of health, medicine, and sport; youth and civic organizations; and media.

The broad range of recommendations generated during the conference included the following:
- The public must be made aware of the problem of establishing and maintaining fitness;
- Fitness must be popularized and promoted among youth;
- Research on fitness is needed to decide what kind and how much;
- Out of school programs should include agencies already working in the field (e.g. Boy and Girl Scouts, YMCA);
- Funds for any programs and initiatives should come from private industry, foundations, community chests; a greater share of tax revenues should be allocated to community recreation;
- Schools should have more time, equipment, and personnel for physical education and should focus increased attention on children who are not athletically gifted, rather than on "stars;"
- The standards and prestige of the physical education profession must be raised;
- Community recreational facilities should be increased and better use made of existing facilities;
- All children must have periodic medical examinations;
- Better leadership is needed for physical activity at home, in the school, and in the community, and adults should be role models for physical fitness.
- Girls should have equal opportunities for physical fitness.

On July 16, 1956, President Eisenhower established the President's Council on Youth Fitness (Executive Order 10673); in the same Executive Order, the president called for creation of a Citizens Advisory Committee on the Fitness of American Youth. Eisenhower envisioned the President's Council on Youth Fitness as a catalytic agency that would educate, stimulate, motivate, and encourage local communities and individual Americans to promote and adopt active lifestyles.

President Eisenhower strongly believed that communities and organizations at the grassroots level were the appropriate agents to design programs and implement corrective actions to address the concerns identified at the federal level. The role of the Council would be to sound the alarm and identify concerns, to be a "catalytic agent" to stimulate and encourage action at the grassroots level.

HIGHLIGHTS IN THE HISTORY OF THE PRESIDENT'S COUNCIL ON PHYSICAL FITNESS AND SPORTS

President Dwight D. Eisenhower, 1953–61

As a former military officer, President Dwight D. Eisenhower was sensitive to the need for fitness among the pool of America's potential fighting forces and was familiar with the complaints of recruiters and officers in the armed forces about the poor fitness levels of American draftees during World War II and the Korean War. At that time, a reported 50 percent of men who showed up at draft boards throughout the nation were considered physically unfit. President Eisenhower was also concerned about the growing problem of juvenile delinquency and considered physical exercise an important measure to keep youth on the playground and off the streets. Sensitive to the appropriate roles of "home and local community," President Eisenhower envisioned parents, schools, and local organizations as the ones to oversee the activities of American children.

The first President's Council on Youth Fitness was chaired by Vice President Nixon; Council members were Cabinet secretaries of the Departments of Interior; Agriculture; Labor; Health, Education and Welfare; and the Attorney General. Funding for Council activities came from the agencies. The Citizens Advisory Committee on the Fitness of American Youth was envisioned as a group of key citizens from a variety of disciplines, whose assignment was to study the problem and to alert the American people about what should be done to achieve the goal of a fit American youth.

As the Cabinet-level members of the Council and Citizens Advisory Committee continued to define and refine their roles and responsibilities during the early years, Interior Secretary Fred A. Seaton, chairman of the Council in 1958, reiterated President Eisenhower's vision of the structure and limitations of the Council, which would be a "stimulator, a catalyst."

By calling attention to the poor state of youth fitness, President Eisenhower set a serious tone for the Council and outlined limited parameters for the organization rather than dictating specific actions and programs from the top down. His view was that it was the role of the federal government to sound the alarm and identify concerns, to be a "catalytic agent" to stimulate and encourage the action at the grassroots level. The function of the Council would be to persuade and educate the American people to do something about fitness, not to dictate policy. To that end, the president sent his Council administrator, Shane McCarthy, around the nation to speak to Americans about the importance of physical fitness.

President John F. Kennedy, 1961–1963

Shortly before he took office, President-elect John F. Kennedy identified physical fitness as a defining principle of his administration. The first media-savvy president to campaign extensively on television, the president-elect mobilized the power of the mainstream media by publishing an article, "The Soft American," in Sports Illustrated (Dec. 26, 1960) less than a month before his inauguration. It was a first—a president-elect writing an article in the popular media to announce public policy before taking office.

In his Sports Illustrated piece, President Kennedy outlined four points as the basis of his physical fitness program: a White House Committee on Health and Fitness; direct oversight of the initiative by the Department of Health, Education and Welfare; an annual Youth Fitness Conference to be attended by state governors; and an unambiguous assertion that physical fitness was the business of the federal government. He concluded the article by laying the foundation for reorganizing the Council. Within a month of his inauguration, President Kennedy spoke at the Conference on Physical Fitness of Youth. Under President Kennedy, the President's Council would not only spread the word to Americans about the importance of physical fitness for youth but would also conduct youth fitness surveys, publish fitness information, and offer technical advice to schools and communities about how to improve physical fitness not only for youth but for Americans of all ages.

Although the Council did not have the authority to impose a national physical fitness program, state and local leaders indicated to the Council that they would welcome guidance. President Kennedy selected Charles ("Bud") Wilkinson, athletic director and football coach at the University of Oklahoma, as the first Physical Fitness Consultant to the President. Wilkinson assembled a professional staff that included Richard Snider (administrator), C. Carson Conrad, and Glenn Swengros.

The Council developed a physical fitness curriculum in consultation with major educational and medical organizations, and published and distributed hundreds of thousands of free publications, including "Youth Physical Fitness" (the "Blue Book") in 1961. In1962, Kennedy published a second article in Sports Illustrated ("The Vigor We Need"). The booklet "Adult Physical Fitness" was published in 1963. That year, a committee was formed by the Council to determine the organization's role in research. Two documents resulted: "Physical Fitness Research Needs" and "Proposed Physical Fitness Research Projects."

When President Kennedy unearthed an old executive order dating back to Theodore Roosevelt, which challenged Marine officers to walk 50 miles in 20 hours, he challenged the White House staff to take a 50-mile hike. As a lark, Attorney General Robert Kennedy accepted the challenge and walked the 50 miles wearing leather oxford shoes. American citizens (mistakenly) thought the president had challenged the public to undertake 50-mile hikes. The Council office quickly explained that while walking for exercise was encouraged, the Council was not sponsoring or rewarding 50-mile hikes.

But the public response to the perceived challenge from the president signaled that the Council's physical fitness message was hitting home and gave the Council legitimacy among its most important audience: average Americans. The country readily embraced a public awareness campaign promoting physical fitness by the National Advertising Council, which blanketed 650 television stations and 3,500 radio stations. Even Peanuts creator Charles Schulz and other cartoonists joined the campaign by promoting exercise in cartoon strips.

Aging boomers today recall exercising to "Chicken Fat," a fun song performed by Robert Preston and written by "The Music Man" himself, Meredith Willson, to support the popular cause of physical fitness.

A million school children took part in Council-sponsored pilot projects to test children's fitness levels. Numerous other national projects were developed, including state demonstration centers to serve as a showcase for model elementary and secondary physical education programs. Other projects included clinics and the production of educational films and booklets.

Although both youth and adult fitness had been the focus of the Council's mission throughout the Kennedy administration, during his final year in office, the president officially expanded the Council's mission to include Americans of all ages (Executive Order 11074, Jan. 9, 1963) and renamed the organization the President's Council on Physical Fitness.

President Lyndon B. Johnson, 1963–69

President Lyndon B. Johnson went forward with the Council programs put in place during the Kennedy administration. President Johnson initially appointed baseball star Stan Musial as Consultant to the President on Physical Fitness; when Musial resigned to take a position in professional sports management, the president asked Vice President Hubert Humphrey to serve as both Council chairman and Consultant to the President on Physical Fitness. President Johnson later appointed Capt. James A. Lovell, U.S. Navy, an astronaut for the National Aeronautics and Space Administration (NASA), to be Consultant to the President on Physical Fitness. President Johnson's Council was the last to have the Cabinet secretaries serve as its members.

To collect data for development of new norms for youth aged 10 to 17, the Council conducted the second national fitness survey in 1964. Based on the results of the survey, the Council established its longstanding award for youth fitness, the beginning of its signature program.

Established in 1966, the Presidential Physical Fitness Award for exceptional achievement was originally administered by the American Alliance of Health, Physical Education and Recreation (AAHPER). The award recognized children in good academic standing who scored in the upper 15th percentile on activities such as a softball throw, a broad jump, a 50-yard dash, and a 600-yard walk/run.

President Johnson strongly believed that participation in sports was an important part of physical fitness. In 1968, he expanded the Council's mandate to include sports and renamed the Council the President's Council on Physical Fitness and Sports (Executive Order 11398). The Council undertook the supervision of the National Summer Youth Sports Program, which provided sports instruction, competition, nutritious lunches, and medical screening for disadvantaged youth. Located on college campuses, the program was administered by the National Collegiate Athletic Association, under Council supervision.

Convinced that fitness was a major health issue, President Johnson broadened the Council's role to include conducting cooperative programs with the medical professions to stimulate research. The Council increasingly provided technical assistance to school systems and departments of education to improve health and fitness programs.

Near the end of his term, President Johnson moved the Council from the White House to the U.S. Department of Health, Education and Welfare (later renamed the U.S. Department of Health and Human Services), where it remains today.

President Richard M. Nixon, 1969–74

When Richard Nixon was elected president in 1968, Capt. James A. Lovell followed protocol and turned in his resignation so that the new president could appoint his own consultant. Nixon invited Lovell to stay on both as Consultant to the President and as Chairman of the Council. It was a year before Lovell's famous Apollo 13 flight.

Lovell recommended that the president appoint physical fitness experts and athletes to be members of the Council. This recommendation was enthusiastically supported by health and fitness organizations, sports professionals, and physical educators.

In 1970 (Executive Order 11562), President Nixon eliminated the Cabinet structure of the Council and created a council comprised of 15 nationally-recognized fitness and sports figures as members, with Lovell as chairman. President Nixon gave the Council a new charter, and the position of executive director was created. The

Council was given an executive director and a professional staff that included V.L. Nicholson, Glenn V. Swengros, and Dr. Richard Keelor. The Council also appointed special advisors in 1970, to stimulate the development of physical fitness programs for employees, enhance public relations activities, and explore the possibility of private support for Council projects.

During the Nixon administration (1971), the Council published the first issue of Physical Fitness Research Digest, a quarterly edited by research consultant Harrison Clarke. In 1972, the Council created a new award, the Presidential Sports Award, to motivate both youth and adults to commit to long-term participation in sports and fitness activities. The Presidential Physical Fitness Awards school program was expanded to allow use by recreation departments and youth groups such as Scouts and Boys and Girls Clubs as well as school physical education programs. Three conferences on fitness in business and industry were conducted by the Council during President Nixon's administration (1972, 1973, and 1974).

President Nixon was credited with reorganizing the Council and for bringing an executive director and professional staff on board to actualize Council programs. C. Carson ("Casey") Conrad served as the Council's first executive director (1970-84).

President Gerald R. Ford, 1974-77

President Gerald R. Ford was an excellent role model for Americans to emulate. An enthusiastic skier who swam daily, President Ford welcomed the recommendations of his Council, under the leadership of Capt. Lovell, who stressed that physical fitness must be a national priority. Despite the best efforts of the Council, youth fitness tests showed no gains; rejection rates in the armed forces remained high; and the economic costs of poor health were increasing rapidly. Endorsing the Council's goals, objectives, and projects fully, President Ford issued Executive Order 11562 (Oct. 25, 1976), which referred for the first time to the Council's responsibility to assist business, industry, government, and labor organizations in establishing physical fitness programs to promote better health and reduce the costs of physical inactivity. Ford's executive order also emphasized the Council's role in educating the public about the connection between physical activity and good health. C. Carson Conrad was executive director of the Council during the Ford administration.

President James E. Carter, 1977-81

President Jimmy Carter was an outspoken and passionate advocate and role model for physical fitness—he was a regular jogger and walker who also enjoyed tennis and bowling. President Carter made himself readily available to speak about the importance of physical fitness and appeared at Council meetings and conferences. As keynote speaker at the National Conference on Physical Fitness and Sports, President Carter described fitness programs as "the best possible investment in health." C. Carson Conrad was executive director of the Council during the Carter administration.

President Ronald W. Reagan, 1981-89

Although he was the oldest man to serve as the nation's chief executive, President Ronald Reagan took an active role in the physical fitness program of his Council and frequently met with Council members, consultants, advisors, and staff at the White House. President Reagan also appeared in TV and print advertising campaigns promoting fitness and sent a taped message to an awards dinner for the National Fitness Foundation in New York. What was arguably his most influential contribution was his appointment of dynamic and proactive NFL coach George Allen (1981-87) as chairman of the Council. In response to Allen's recommendations, President Reagan issued Executive Order 12399 (Dec. 31, 1982), which called for the Council to do the following:

- enlist the active support and assistance of individual citizens, civic groups, private enterprise, voluntary organizations, and others in efforts to promote and improve the fitness of all Americans through regular participation in physical fitness and sports activities;
- initiate programs to inform the general public of the importance of exercise and the link between regular physical activity, good health, and effective performance;
- strengthen coordination of federal services and programs relating to physical fitness and sports participation and invite appropriate federal agencies to participate in an interagency committee to coordinate physical fitness and sports activities within the federal government;
- encourage state and local governments to emphasize the importance of regular physical fitness and sports participation;
- seek to advance the physical fitness of children, youth, adults, and senior citizens by systematically encouraging the development of community recreation, physical fitness, and sports participation programs;

- develop cooperative programs with medical, dental, and other similar professional societies to encourage the implementation of sound physical fitness practices and sports medicine services;
- stimulate and encourage research in the areas of sports medicine, physical fitness, and sports performance;
- assist educational agencies at all levels in developing high-quality, innovative health and physical education programs that emphasize the importance of exercise to good health;
- assist recreation agencies and national sports governing bodies at all levels in developing "sports for all" programs to emphasize the value of sports to physical, mental, and emotional fitness;
- assist business, industry, government, and labor organizations in establishing sound physical fitness programs to elevate employee fitness and reduce the financial and human costs resulting from physical inactivity.

Ever the enthusiastic coach and motivator throughout his six-year tenure as chairman, Allen stimulated the Council to stretch, to imagine all possibilities and make them happen. Under his leadership, the Council established regional sports clinics and private-sector employee programs; established programs to inform the general public of the importance of exercise and the link between regular physical activity, good health, and effective performance; conducted public service advertising campaigns (usually two major media campaigns a year); worked with the U.S. Postal Service to issue a physical fitness postage stamp; published a Council newsletter; published numerous public information materials in cosponsorship with private companies and groups; established Governors' Councils on Physical Fitness, State Demonstration Centers, and State Games; established the State Champion program recognizing schools with the highest percentage of students earning awards; expanded activities for the Presidential Sports Award; cosponsored medical symposiums for physicians and physical educators, which focused on the role of exercise in disease prevention; organized the National Fitness Coalition, a cooperative effort by the Council, the National Recreation and Parks Association, and the National Association of Governors' Councils; and initiated National Physical Fitness and Sports Month, encouraging local communities to increase participation in sports and fitness activities such as fitness fairs, fun walks and runs, media events, and panel discussions.

Other initiatives spearheaded by Allen and the other Reagan administration Council members were the National Fitness Foundation; the U.S. Fitness Academy; the National Fitness Classic; the Adult Fitness Card; the National Fitness Testing Week; and Youth Fitness Forums.

During the Reagan administration, the Council appointed 44 special advisors. In 1983, the Council hosted the White House Symposium on Physical Fitness and Sports Medicine and proclaimed May as National Physical Fitness and Sports Month. In 1984, the Council sponsored the National Conference on Youth Fitness; held six regional public hearings on physical fitness and physical education; and sponsored the first National Women's Leadership Conference on Fitness, with the first lady as honorary chair.

During that period, the Council, in cooperation with the American Alliance of Health, Physical Education, Recreation and Dance (AAHPERD), introduced a program known as "Fitnessgram," based on the AAHPERD National Youth Fitness Test. The program was developed by the Institute for Aerobic Research and funded by the Campbell Soup Company. A pilot study was conducted in Oklahoma during the 1982-83 school year and expanded the following year.

In 1985, the National School Population Fitness Survey was conducted, the last survey of its kind by the Council. This resulted in the establishment of a new award, the National Physical Fitness Award, to recognize children who scored between the 50th and 85th percentiles on the Presidential Physical Fitness Test, as well as children who performed at the 85th percentile and above, who continued to receive the Presidential Physical Fitness Award.

By the mid-1980s, the youth fitness test had five components: sit-ups; pull-ups, push-ups, or flexed-arm hang to measure upper body strength; a one-mile walk/run; a V-sit reach; and the shuttle run. In 1986, the Council adopted the name "President's Challenge Youth Physical Fitness Awards Program" for its youth physical fitness testing. In 1988, the Amateur Athletic Union (AAU), in collaboration with the University of Indiana School of Health, Physical Education, and Recreation (HPER), became the administrator of the President's Challenge program.

One of the most popular initiatives undertaken by the Reagan administration was the Healthy American Fitness Leaders Awards (1984-96). The annual awards banquet, cosponsored by Allstate Insurance and the Junior Chamber of Commerce (Jaycees), recognized 10 outstanding fitness leaders each year. The awardees eventually formed the National Fitness Leaders Association (NFLA), headquartered in Washington, D.C.

C. Carson Conrad served as executive director during President Reagan's first term; Asahel E. ("Ash") Hayes was executive director from 1984-89.

George H.W. Bush, 1989-93

By appointing Arnold Schwarzenegger as his Council chairman, President George H. W. Bush achieved a level of recognition and popular awareness of the Council unseen since the days of President Kennedy. "Arnold" (as everyone called the chairman) understood how to use the celebrity gained as a body builder (seven-time winner of Mr. Olympia) and as a Hollywood film star to give maximum exposure to the Council and its messages. On his own initiative and at his own expense, Schwarzenegger traveled to all 50 states to advocate personally to governors the need for daily, quality physical education in American schools.

GREAT AMERICAN WORKOUTS. During Schwarzenegger's tenure as chairman, National Physical Fitness and Sports Month became a nationally televised celebration, when President and Mrs. Bush joined Arnold and other celebrity athletes and Hollywood personalities at "Great American Workouts" held on the White House lawn during President Bush's administration.

Council administrative changes under the Bush administration included an increase in the number of Council members from 15 to 20, and an increased emphasis on public–private collaborations on physical fitness programs and initiatives.

In 1989, the Council was named lead agency on the physical activity and fitness priority area of the government report, "Healthy People 2000," published every 10 years by the HHS Office of Disease Prevention and Health Promotion; the Centers for Disease Control and Prevention (CDC) served as science advisor.

During the administration of President George H.W. Bush, Wilmer "Vinegar Bend" Mizell (1989-91) and John Butterfield (1991-93) served as executive directors.

William J. Clinton, 1993-2001

President Bill Clinton appointed Florence Griffith Joyner ("Flo Jo") and Tom McMillen as Council co-chairs. Olympic track and field medalist Griffith Joyner was both the first woman and the first African American to serve in a Council leadership position. After McMillen's retirement from the Council and Griffith Joyner's untimely death, President Clinton appointed Lee Haney, body builder and eight-time Mr. Olympia winner, as Council chair (1999-2002). Haney was the first African American to serve as sole Council chair.

In 1993, the Council conducted a Strategic Planning Forum to discuss an adult fitness survey and obtain recommendations on how to improve physical activity and fitness among Americans. Under a partnership with the Advil Foundation, "The Nolan Ryan Fitness Guide" was made available to over 850,000 Americans. In 1994, the Council established the Silver Eagle Award to promote fitness among seniors. That same year, the Council began publishing a quarterly periodical, the PCPFS Physical Activity and Fitness Research Digest.

GET UP, GET OUT CAMPAIGN. In 1995, the Council partnered with the Sporting Goods Manufacturing Association (SGMA), the International Health and Raquet Sportsclub Association (IHRSA), and the Advertising Council ("Ad Council") to develop a three-year public awareness campaign focusing on youth fitness. Under the catchy slogans "Get Off It" and "Get Up, Get Out," the cutting edge campaign featured spots promoting exercise to sedentary, overweight adults and children.

FLEXING THE NATION'S MUSCLE. In 1996, in partnership with the National Archives and Records Administration, the Council cosponsored "Flexing the Nation's Muscle: Presidents, Physical Fitness and Sports in the American Century," a traveling exhibit about physical activity and fitness among 20th century presidents. The exhibit traveled to presidential libraries around the country before being retired and stored at the Truman Library.

In the mid-1990s, the Council moved its offices to the headquarters of the U.S. Department of Health and Human Services (HHS) and became an increasingly important component of HHS, within the Office of the Assistant Secretary for Health (ASH), Office of Public Health and Science (OPHS). During this period, studies increasingly revealed the scientific basis for the role played by physical activity and fitness in disease prevention and overall good health.

HEALTHY PEOPLE 2010 AND PHYSICAL ACTIVITY AND HEALTH: A REPORT OF THE SURGEON GENERAL. During the Clinton administration, the President's Council on Physical Fitness and Sports served as co-lead with the CDC in developing physical activity and fitness objectives for Healthy People 2010, the government's statement of goals and objectives for the next decade, and as co-lead in the Surgeon General's report "Physical Activity and Health."

The publication in 1996 of the Surgeon General's landmark report signaled a major shift in the way physical fitness was viewed and discussed by the general public as well as health and fitness professionals. Now "physical activity" joined "physical fitness" as a recognized essential for good health. Among the findings reported in "Physical Activity and Health" are

- People of all ages, both male and female, benefit from regular physical activity;
- Significant health benefits can be obtained by including a moderate amount of physical activity (e.g. 30

minutes of brisk walking or raking leaves, 15 minutes of running, or 45 minutes of playing volleyball) on most, if not all, days of the week. Through a modest increase in daily activity, most Americans can improve their health and quality of life.
- Additional health benefits can be gained through greater amounts of physical activity. People who can maintain a regular regimen of activity that is of longer duration or of more vigorous intensity are likely to derive greater benefit;
- Physical activity reduces the risk of premature mortality in general and of coronary heart disease, hypertension, colon cancer, and type 2 diabetes in particular. Physical activity also improves mental health and is important for the health of muscles, bones, and joints.
- Research on understanding and promoting physical activity is at an early stage, but some interventions to promote physical activity through schools, worksites, and healthcare settings have been evaluated and found to be successful.

PHYSICAL ACTIVITY AND SPORT IN THE LIVES OF GIRLS. In 1997, the Council published a report, "Physical Activity and Sport in the Lives of Girls," under the direction of the Center for Research on Girls and Women in Sport, University of Minnesota. The report described the status of physical activity and sports for women and girls in athletics, discussed the impact of Title IX, and recommended further ways to promote physical activity and sports opportunities for women and girls, noting that young females were twice as likely to be inactive as young males.

PROMOTING BETTER HEALTH FOR YOUNG PEOPLE THROUGH PHYSICAL ACTIVITY AND SPORTS. In 2000, President Clinton issued an Executive Memorandum, directing the secretaries of the U.S. Department of Health and Human Services and the U.S. Department of Education to identify strategies to improve the nation's youth fitness. The report, "Promoting Better Health For Young People through Physical Activity and Sports," was submitted to the president in November 2000.

WWW.FITNESS.GOV. In January 2001, shortly before President Clinton left office, the Council launched www.fitness.gov, a gateway Web site to the vast government information resources available on physical activity, fitness and health.

During the Clinton administration, Sandra Perlmutter was the Council's executive director, the first woman to serve in that position (1993-2001).

President George W. Bush

President George W. Bush signed Executive Order 13265 on June 6, 2002, reinvigorating the Council and reaffirming its role in advising and assisting the president and the secretary of Health and Human Services in expanding national awareness of the health benefits of regular physical activity and sports.

On June 20, 2002, President Bush introduced his President's Council on Physical Fitness and Sports at a fitness festival and expo on the South Lawn of the White House. In appointing NFL Hall of Fame winner and four-time Super Bowl champion Lynn C. Swann as chairman, and Olympic Softball gold medalist and orthopedic surgeon Dr. Dorothy G. ("Dot") Richardson as vice chair, the president recognized their value as dynamic role models and national spokespersons.

Highly sought-after motivational speakers, Swann and Richardson took the president's health and physical activity messages to audiences nationwide through conference presentations and media appearances.

The other members of Bush's Council included professional athletes, U.S. Olympians, physicians, educators, organization leaders, and corporate executives.

HealthierUS. When he introduced his Council, President Bush also launched his HealthierUS initiative, based on the premise that anyone can improve health by adopting four basic behaviors:

- Be physically active every day.
- Eat a nutritious diet.
- Get preventive screenings.
- Make healthy choices/avoid risky behaviors

PREVENTION. During the Bush administration, the president, HHS secretaries, the Surgeon General, and the Council members stressed a uniform message: prevention is key to overcoming the nation's health problems. Swann and Richardson testified before several congressional committees about the health benefits of physical activity.

In 2001, the Council introduced a new award, the Presidential Active Lifestyle Award (PALA), developed as a response to the key findings of the 1996 Surgeon General's Report on Physical Activity and Health.

THE PRESIDENT'S CHALLENGE GROWS UP. On Jan. 15, 2003, Council Chairman Lynn Swann announced at the National Press Club that for the first time, the President's Challenge awards program would be offered to adults as well as youth. Swann announced that the Presidential Active Lifestyle Award (PALA) was now available to adults, including seniors, as well as children and teens. Americans of all ages could earn a PALA by being active 30 to 60 minutes a day, five days a week for six weeks.

WWW.PresidentsChallenge.ORG. A few months later (July 18, 2003), President Bush and Swann launched www.presidentschallenge.org, the Council's interactive physical activity and fitness online program. The new President's Challenge offered an award for active lifestyles (PALA) and for points logged toward earning medals (Presidential Champions award). The more than 100 activities included in the program range from traditional sports and activities, such as walking, running, swimming, baseball and soccer, to yoga, tai chi, dancing, housework, and gardening.

The President's Challenge interactive Web site was designed to be highly adaptable for individuals, families, schools, after school programs, clubs, workplace wellness programs, sports and fitness facilities, senior centers, and other groups. The federal government was among the first to utilize the President's Challenge Web site for an employee health program. In fall 2003, HHS Secretary Tommy Thompson announced the Secretary's Challenge, an HHS employee physical activity program using the group feature of the President's Challenge Web site. In fall 2004, HHS and the Office of Personnel Management (OPM) launched the HealthierFeds Physical Activity Challenge for federal employees. Over 30,000 federal employees from 30 agencies participated.

The HHS Office on Disability used the PALA as part of its "I Can Do It, You Can Do It" program to provide adult mentors to children with disabilities, in order to encourage the kids to become active. The Council also partnered with the HHS Administration on Aging's (AoA) "You Can" program to encourage older Americans to take the President's Challenge.

The Web site was adapted for the Wisconsin Governor's Challenge program, launched to motivate citizens of Wisconsin to use the President's Challenge program to become regularly active.

Over 80 corporations, nonprofit organizations, and medical and educational institutions became President's Challenge Advocates during the Web site's first three years, utilizing or sponsoring the President's Challenge program in schools and in the workplace.

THE PCPFS SCIENCE BOARD AND SCIENCE PARTNERS. To bring the best available scientific expertise to the Council, the President's Council Science Board was established in 2003. In addition to appointing individual Science Board members, science partnerships were established with the American College of Sports Medicine, the National Strength and Conditioning Association, and the National Athletic Trainers Association.

REVITALIZING NATIONAL PHYSICAL FITNESS AND SPORTS MONTH. In 2004, 2005, and 2006, President Bush issued presidential proclamations calling on all Americans to observe National Physical Fitness and Sports Month, "May Month." Recalling the "Great American Workouts" held in the early 1990s, the Council of President George W. Bush hosted the HealthierUS Fitness Festival on the National Mall in 2004 and 2005, and the HealthierUS Fitness Challenge at RFK Stadium in 2006, which featured the kickoff of the HealthierUS Veterans program.

Lisa Oliphant was executive director from 2001–02; Capt. Penelope Royall was acting executive director from 2002–03; Melissa Johnson has served as executive director since 2003.

FIFTY YEARS OF ACTIVATING AMERICANS

About 1980, the health and physical fitness of Americans began a downward spiral, as the rates of overweight and obesity began to climb. The nation now faces a growing public health epidemic, one that threatens the well-being of future generations. As the nation has become more urbanized, motorized, and screen-centered, an increasing number of people lead sedentary lives, and the rates of overweight and obesity continue to soar. The United States has the highest prevalence of obesity in the world.

The children of the 1950s, whose performance on fitness tests shocked President Eisenhower and caused him to establish the President's Council on Youth Fitness, as well as the kids who exercised to the "Chicken Fat" song in the 1960s, are now among the two-thirds of American adults who are overweight or obese. Their children and grandchildren are among 9 million overweight American youth, some of whom are developing type 2 diabetes at as young an age as 8. These are the challenges faced by the President's Council on Physical Fitness and Sports as it enters its next 50 years and charts its future.

For 50 years, the Council has remained constant in adhering to President Eisenhower's original vision—to serve as a stimulator and a catalyst. By activating resources within the public, private, and nonprofit spheres of American life, the President's Council on Physical Fitness and Sports continues to confront a pressing health problem, sedentary behavior, in creative ways that allow for both bipartisanship and continuity.